Navigating the AI Job Market: How to Future-Proof Your Career

Frank Zanish

Contents

Chapter One

Decoding the AI Job Market

UNDERSTANDING THE CURRENT LANDSCAPE OF THE AI JOB MARKET

The world is in the midst of a technological revolution, and one field that is at the forefront of this transformation is Artificial Intelligence (AI). As AI continues to advance at an unprecedented pace, it has revolutionized various industries, creating new opportunities and challenges for job seekers. In this chapter, we will delve into the current landscape of the AI job market, exploring its rapid growth, analyzing its impact on traditional job roles, and discussing the evolving skill sets required for AI careers.

The Rapid Growth of the AI Job Market

In recent years, there has been a surge in demand for professionals with AI skills across industries. The exponential growth can be attributed to several factors such as advancements in technology, increased data availability, and growing recognition of AI's potential to drive innovation and efficiency. From healthcare to finance to manufacturing, organizations are harnessing the power of AI to automate processes, gain insights from data analytics, and improve decision-making.

Impact on Traditional Job Roles

As organizations adopt AI technologies, traditional job roles are undergoing significant transformations. Repetitive tasks that were once performed by humans are now being automated by machines equipped with sophisticated algorithms. This shift requires individuals to adapt their skill sets and embrace new roles that complement these technological advancements. While some fear that AI will eliminate jobs entirely, it is important to note that it also creates new opportunities for individuals who possess both technical expertise in AI and domain knowledge in specific industries.

Evolving Skill Sets for AI Careers

To thrive in today's competitive job market influenced by AI technology, professionals need to continuously update their skill sets. While technical skills such as machine learning algorithms or programming languages like Python are essential foundations for an aspiring AI professional; critical thinking skills have also become crucial. The ability to analyze complex datasets objectively and make informed decisions based on those insights is highly valued by employers.

Challenges and Opportunities in the AI Job Market

While the demand for AI professionals is high, there are challenges that job seekers must navigate. One such challenge is the rapid pace at which AI technology evolves. Staying abreast of the latest developments and continuously learning new skills can be daunting. Additionally, ethical considerations surrounding AI, such as data privacy and bias mitigation, require professionals to be well-versed in responsible and ethical practices. However, amidst these challenges lie tremendous opportunities for those willing to embrace them. The growing need for AI professionals has created a competitive market with attractive salaries and benefits. Moreover, by mastering the essential skills demanded in this field, individuals can position themselves as valuable assets to organizations seeking to leverage AI technologies.

In this section, we have explored the current landscape of the AI job market. We have witnessed how organizations across industries are increasingly incorporating AI into their operations and how this transformation impacts traditional job roles. We have also discussed the evolving skill sets required for success in an AI career and examined both the challenges and opportunities that exist within this dynamic field.

IDENTIFYING THE DEMAND FOR AI SKILLS ACROSS INDUSTRIES

The world is witnessing a technological revolution, and at the heart of this transformation lies artificial intelligence (AI). As AI continues to advance at an unprecedented pace, it has become crucial to understand how different industries are incorporating this groundbreaking technology into their operations. In this chapter, we will explore the importance of identifying industry-specific demand for AI skills and delve into the strategies that can enhance your career prospects in this rapidly evolving job market.

Exploring Industry Integration

Industries across the board are recognizing the potential of AI to revolutionize their processes and drive innovation. From healthcare to finance, retail to transportation, AI is making its presence felt everywhere. Let's take a closer look at how some key industries are incorporating AI into their operations. In healthcare, AI is being used to analyze vast amounts of patient data and develop personalized treatment plans. It can assist doctors in diagnosing diseases more accurately and enable researchers to make significant breakthroughs in medical research.

The finance industry is leveraging AI algorithms for fraud detection, risk assessment, and algorithmic trading. These technologies have not only improved efficiency but also enhanced security measures within financial institutions. Retail giants are utilizing machine learning algorithms to analyze customer behavior patterns and provide personalized shopping experiences. Chatbots powered by natural language processing have transformed customer support services by providing instant assistance round-the-clock. Transportation companies are utilizing self-driving vehicles that rely on computer vision systems powered by deep learning algorithms. This technology has immense potential to reduce accidents and increase fuel efficiency in road transportation.

Identifying High-Demand Industries

Now that we have explored how various industries are integrating AI into their operations let's focus on identifying key industries with a high demand for AI professionals. These industries present excellent career opportunities for those seeking a future-proof career in the field of artificial intelligence.

1. **Healthcare**: With an increasing emphasis on personalized medicine and innovative healthcare solutions, the demand for AI professionals in the healthcare industry is soaring. Roles such as medical data analysts, bioinformatics specialists, and AI research scientists are in high demand.

2. **Finance**: The finance industry heavily relies on data analysis and risk assessment. As a result, professionals with expertise in AI algorithms, machine learning, and predictive modeling are highly sought after. Job roles such as financial analysts, quantitative researchers, and algorithmic traders are at the forefront of this demand.

3. **Retail**: E-commerce platforms and brick-and-mortar retailers alike are investing heavily in AI-driven technologies to enhance customer experiences and optimize supply chain management. Job roles like data scientists, marketing analysts, and consumer behavior experts are witnessing a surge in demand within the retail sector.

4. **Manufacturing**: In an era of Industry 4.0, manufacturers are embracing automation and robotics powered by AI to streamline production processes and improve efficiency levels. This has led to an increased demand for experts in robotic process automation (RPA), machine vision programming, and industrial optimization.

Aligning Skills with Industry Demands

To maximize your career prospects within the AI job market, it is essential to align your skills with specific industry demands effectively. One way to accomplish this is by **staying updated** with the latest trends and advancements within your desired industry. **Continuous**

learning plays a vital role in staying ahead of the curve. Online courses specializing in AI applications within different industries can help you acquire new skills or deepen existing ones. Additionally, gaining relevant certifications can provide tangible proof of your expertise to potential employers.

Building a **strong professional network** within the AI community can also open doors to exciting opportunities within high-demand industries. Attending conferences or joining industry-specific forums enables you to connect with like-minded individuals who share valuable insights into current trends and job prospects.

EMBRACING THE RISE OF AI AND ROBOTICS

In this section, we delve into the captivating world of careers intertwined with the ever-evolving domains of artificial intelligence and robotics. Brace yourself for a mind-bending exploration filled with endless possibilities and thrilling prospects. As we embark on this exhilarating journey, let us unlock the secrets to not only surviving but thriving in an era where machines become our steadfast companions. Imagine a future where robots gracefully navigate our bustling cities, their metallic hands deftly crafting intricate designs that surpass even the wildest dreams of human ingenuity. Picture yourself at the forefront of this technological revolution, as you harness your skills and knowledge to shape a world teeming with limitless potential. The realm of AI and robotics beckons, my dear reader, offering countless avenues for those brave enough to seize them.

As we plunge deeper into this chapter's pulsating core, it is crucial to emphasize that while automation may replace certain tasks traditionally performed by humans, it simultaneously opens up new frontiers brimming with opportunities for innovation and creativity. The key lies in embracing change rather than fearing it; adapting our skill sets to complement the burgeoning capabilities of intelligent machines. To truly thrive in this brave new world, one must cultivate a multidisciplinary mindset that transcends conventional boundaries. Gone are the days when narrow expertise sufficed; now is the time for **polymaths** - individuals who possess a diverse range of skills across various domains - to take center stage. As you embark upon your journey towards embracing AI and robotics, remember that versatility is your most powerful weapon.

The fusion between humans and machines grants birth to remarkable career paths previously unimaginable. Imagine becoming an AI ethicist - an individual responsible for ensuring ethical guidelines are woven seamlessly into every line of code governing artificial intelligence systems. Or perhaps you yearn to explore uncharted territories as a robot psychologist - delving deep into their mechanical minds to understand their emotions, motivations, and inner workings. But the allure of careers in AI and robotics extends far beyond these fascinating niches. The fields of computer vision, machine learning, and natural language processing beckon with their siren call. Unlocking the secrets of autonomous vehicles, creating groundbreaking medical technologies that revolutionize healthcare as we know it - the possibilities are as vast as the cosmos itself.

As you navigate this labyrinthine landscape of opportunities, remember that continuous learning is your trusty compass. Stay abreast of emerging technologies and immerse yourself in lifelong education. Seek out internships, workshops, and mentorships to sharpen your skills and gain invaluable hands-on experience. Embrace failure as a stepping stone towards growth, for it is through setbacks that we uncover our true potential.

My dear reader, we stand on the precipice of an unprecedented era where humans dance in harmonious syncopation with machines. The opportunities within the realm of AI and robotics stretch out before us like a captivating tapestry awaiting our vibrant brushstrokes. Let us embrace this future together - a symphony woven from the threads of human ingenuity and technological marvels. And so I leave you with these words: be bold in your pursuits; let curiosity be your guiding light. For within this ever-shifting landscape lies a world ripe with possibilities - where careers intertwine effortlessly with AI and robotics to birth a new era unlike any other. Together, let us forge ahead into this brave new frontier and carve our destinies amidst the hum of intelligent machines.

RECOGNIZING THE KEY DRIVERS SHAPING THE FUTURE OF AI CAREERS

As we delve deeper into the world of artificial intelligence (AI), it becomes crucial to understand the key drivers that are shaping the future of AI careers. In this chapter, we will explore how advancements in technology, changing consumer behavior, government initiatives, emerging technologies, ethical considerations and regulations, and global trends are influencing and transforming the landscape of AI careers.

Advancements in Technology

The rapid pace at which technology is advancing has a profound impact on AI careers. Breakthroughs in machine learning algorithms, natural language processing techniques, and robotics have opened up new avenues for professionals with expertise in these areas. For example, machine learning enables computers to learn from data without being explicitly programmed, while natural language processing allows machines to understand and process human language. These advancements create exciting opportunities for individuals skilled in these fields to contribute to cutting-edge projects across industries.

Changing Consumer Behavior

Consumer behavior is another significant driver shaping the future of AI careers. As consumers increasingly interact with intelligent virtual assistants like Siri or Alexa and rely on recommendation systems for personalized experiences online, businesses are recognizing the need for AI expertise. Professionals who can analyze vast amounts of data and develop algorithms that understand consumer behavior patterns will be highly sought after by companies looking to optimize their products or services.

Government Initiatives

Governments around the world are realizing the potential of AI as a catalyst for economic growth and societal development. Many countries are investing heavily in research and development initiatives related to AI technologies. These government-driven efforts not only fuel innovation but also create a demand for skilled professionals within their borders. As governments continue to prioritize investments in AI infrastructure and talent development programs, individuals who possess specialized knowledge can expect a growing number of career opportunities.

Ethical Considerations and Regulations

The rise of AI also brings forth ethical considerations that need careful examination. Concerns regarding data privacy, bias mitigation algorithms, and the responsible use of AI technologies are at the forefront of discussions. Regulatory frameworks are being developed to ensure that AI is used ethically and responsibly. Professionals who can navigate these ethical challenges and develop AI solutions that align with societal values will play a crucial role in shaping the future of AI careers.

Global Trends

The field of AI transcends borders, allowing for international collaboration and talent migration. Global trends such as collaborations between countries, knowledge sharing, and talent exchange shape the opportunities available to individuals seeking AI careers. Professionals who possess a global mindset, cultural adaptability, and cross-cultural communication skills will have a competitive advantage in this interconnected world.

Chapter Two

Essential AI Skills for Career Success

MASTERING ESSENTIAL SKILLS FOR SUCCESS IN AN EVOLVING JOB MARKET

In the ever-evolving landscape of the AI job market, it is crucial to possess a set of essential skills that can propel your career forward. As technology continues to advance at a rapid pace, professionals must adapt and cultivate these skills to stay relevant and competitive. This chapter will delve into the key skills required for success in an AI-centric job market, exploring their significance and providing real-life examples to illustrate their practical applications.

Technical Skills: The Foundation of AI Excellence

At the core of any successful career in artificial intelligence lies a solid foundation of technical skills. Proficiency in programming languages such as Python, R, and Java is essential for developing algorithms, implementing machine learning models, and analyzing data. Additionally, knowledge of statistical techniques and data visualization tools enables professionals to extract meaningful insights from vast amounts of information.

Consider Sarah, an aspiring data scientist who dreams of revolutionizing healthcare through AI-driven solutions. With her strong programming background and expertise in machine learning algorithms, she develops predictive models that assist doctors in diagnosing diseases at an early stage. Sarah's technical prowess allows her to harness the power of AI to make a tangible impact on patient outcomes.

Critical Thinking: Navigating Complex Challenges
In an evolving job market influenced by AI technology, critical thinking is paramount. Professionals must possess the ability to analyze complex problems from various angles and develop innovative solutions. By leveraging logical reasoning and creativity, individuals can uncover patterns within datasets or identify areas where AI can streamline processes.

Imagine John, a business analyst tasked with optimizing supply chain operations for a global e-commerce company. Through his keen analytical skills combined with his understanding of AI applications like robotic process automation (RPA), John identifies inefficiencies within warehouse management systems. By implementing intelligent automation solutions powered by RPA bots, he streamlines order fulfillment processes resulting in significant cost savings for the company.

Adaptability: Embracing Change and Continuous Learning

As AI technology continues to evolve, professionals must embrace change and pursue continuous learning to stay ahead. This requires adaptability, a mindset that enables individuals to navigate through uncertainties and acquire new skills as needed. Professionals who can quickly adapt to emerging technologies or industry trends will find themselves in high demand.

Let's meet Alex, a software engineer with a passion for AI. When deep learning emerged as a game-changer in the field, Alex recognized the importance of expanding his skill set. He enrolled in online courses and attended workshops on neural networks and natural language processing. Armed with new knowledge, Alex became instrumental in developing cutting-edge AI applications for his company, securing his position as an indispensable asset.

MASTERING THE LANGUAGE OF AI

In the vast landscape of artificial intelligence, where data reigns supreme and algorithms dance with precision, one must possess a powerful tool to unlock the true potential of this realm. That tool is none other than **programming languages**. Just as a maestro wields his baton to conduct a symphony, so too must we embrace the power of languages like Python and R to compose our own masterpiece in the AI job market. As we delve deeper into the labyrinthine world of AI, it becomes abundantly clear that proficiency in programming languages is not merely desirable but absolutely indispensable. These languages are the very fabric that weaves together intricate algorithms and breathes life into cutting-edge models. Python, with its elegant syntax and extensive libraries, stands as a beacon of versatility in this domain. Meanwhile, R shines as a statistical powerhouse, enabling us to unravel complex data patterns and draw meaningful insights.

To truly harness the power of AI, one must become fluent in these linguistic marvels. Like an artist honing their craft or an alchemist deciphering ancient runes, we must immerse ourselves in the depths of these languages until they become second nature. The journey may seem daunting at first glance, but fear not! For within these pages lies a roadmap that will navigate you through treacherous terrain towards programming mastery.

It all begins with **Python** – a language so dynamic that it seems to breathe fire into even the most mundane lines of code. With its intuitive syntax and vast array of libraries such as TensorFlow and PyTorch, Python empowers us to build neural networks that can conquer mountains of data with ease. From image recognition to natural language processing, Python unlocks limitless possibilities for those willing to venture forth.

In our quest for AI supremacy, let us not overlook **R** – an unsung hero often overshadowed by its more flamboyant counterparts. With its statistical prowess and unrivaled visualization capabilities, R is the language of choice for data scientists seeking to uncover hidden gems within vast oceans of information. Armed with its arsenal of packages like ggplot2 and dplyr, we can transform raw data into meaningful stories that captivate both the mind and the eye.

As we traverse the winding path towards AI proficiency, it is essential to remember that these languages are not mere tools but extensions of our own creative faculties. They grant us the power to mold raw data into actionable insights, to sculpt algorithms that shape our future. It is through this mastery that we become architects of change, wielding code as our medium and innovation as our muse. Thus, dear reader, I implore you to embark on this journey with unwavering determination and unbridled enthusiasm. Embrace Python's elegance and R's finesse as you unravel the mysteries of AI programming. Let your imagination soar as you weave lines of code into intricate tapestries that push the boundaries of what was once thought possible.

Remember, in this ever-evolving landscape where opportunities abound and challenges beckon, those who possess fluency in programming languages shall rise above the rest. So go forth, my fellow explorer of AI's vast frontier; let your passion guide you as you navigate this thrilling job market with newfound confidence. And thus concludes another section in our quest for AI supremacy - filled with wonderment and awe at the limitless potential that awaits those who dare to embrace it. Until next time, dear reader, may your code be elegant and your algorithms revolutionary!

MASTERING THE ART OF DATA SCIENCE AND ANALYTICS FOR AN AI CODING CAREER

In this pivotal chapter, we delve deep into the fascinating realm of data science and analytics, unlocking the secrets to acquiring these essential skills for a well-rounded AI skill set. As we embark on this exhilarating journey, prepare to be captivated by the sheer power and potential that lies within the realm of data. With every passing day, our world becomes increasingly data-driven. From business operations to scientific research, from healthcare to finance, data reigns supreme as the driving force behind innovation and progress. In order to thrive in this rapidly evolving landscape, it is imperative for aspiring AI professionals to master the art of harnessing and analyzing vast amounts of data.

Data science is not merely a buzzword; it is an intricate tapestry interwoven with statistics, mathematics, computer science, and domain expertise. To embark on this quest for knowledge and expertise, one must first understand the fundamental pillars that support this discipline. At its core, data science revolves around extracting meaningful insights from raw information. It requires a unique blend of technical skills such as programming languages (**Python** being a popular choice), **statistical analysis tools** (R or SAS), and **database management systems** (SQL). However, technical prowess alone is not enough; it must be complemented by a solid foundation in mathematics and statistics. Imagine yourself standing at the crossroads where numbers come alive with purpose. Here lies your gateway to unraveling complex patterns hidden within mountains of data through exploratory analysis techniques such as visualization or hypothesis testing. As you traverse these winding paths paved with figures and equations, you will uncover profound truths concealed beneath layers of obscurity.

But let us not confine ourselves solely to the captivating allure of data science. For true mastery in today's AI job market demands an additional set of skills - **analytics**. Analytics empowers us with the ability to transform raw information into actionable insights that drive decision-making processes. It is the bridge that connects data science with real-world applications, enabling organizations to make informed choices and optimize their operations. Within the realm of analytics, lies a world teeming with possibilities. From descriptive analytics that paints vivid pictures of historical trends to predictive analytics that foretells future outcomes, this domain offers a myriad of tools and techniques for unraveling the mysteries hidden within data's embrace.

To truly excel in this field, one must become well-versed in **statistical modeling**, **machine learning algorithms**, and **data visualization**. These skills enable us to unleash the true power of analytics by transforming complex datasets into clear narratives that resonate with decision-makers across diverse industries. As we draw closer to the culmination of this section, it is important to recognize that acquiring data science and analytics skills is not a one-time endeavor but rather an **ongoing pursuit of knowledge**. The landscapes of AI and technology are ever-evolving; what is cutting-edge today may become obsolete tomorrow. Therefore, it is crucial for aspiring professionals in this field to embrace a growth mindset and cultivate a lifelong passion for learning.

Dear reader, as you embark on your own journey towards mastering data science and analytics for a well-rounded AI skill set, remember this: within these realms lie unprecedented opportunities waiting to be seized. With every line of code written or model trained, you inch closer towards shaping the future and carving your mark upon this vast landscape. So let us march forward together into the uncharted territories of data science and analytics - where limitless potential awaits those courageous enough to seek it. Let us unlock the secrets hidden within these intricate tapestries woven from numbers - for they hold the key to navigating the AI job market with confidence and securing our place amidst technological revolutions yet unseen.

Embrace this thrilling odyssey with fervor in your heart and purpose in your step - for you are destined to leave an indelible impact upon this world driven by artificial intelligence.

Chapter Three

The Role of AI Ethicists

THE ETHICAL COMPASS OF AI – The Role of AI Ethicists

In this chapter, dear readers, we delve into the intricate web of ethical considerations that permeate the realm of careers in Artificial Intelligence. Brace yourselves, for we are about to embark on a thought-provoking journey into the role of those who hold the moral compass in this ever-evolving landscape - the **AI Ethicists**. As we traverse this chapter, let us begin by pondering upon the profound impact that AI has on our lives. With each passing day, as technology advances at an exponential pace, questions arise about how these advancements align with our core values and principles. Enter the AI Ethicists - those individuals bestowed with the daunting task of navigating complex dilemmas and ensuring that AI is used ethically and responsibly.

The foremost duty of an AI Ethicist is to **safeguard against biases** embedded within algorithms and systems. Just as a meteorologist predicts a storm brewing on the horizon, these experts identify potential biases lurking within datasets or models before they wreak havoc in real-life scenarios. They act as guardians, protecting society from algorithmic discrimination and injustice. But their influence goes far beyond combating biases alone; they also grapple with weighty moral quandaries. Consider autonomous vehicles faced with a split-second decision: should it prioritize saving its occupants at all costs or protect pedestrians? It is here where AI Ethicists step in and strive to strike a delicate **balance between human lives, ethical principles, and legal implications**. Their task is not for mere mortals but requires intellectual prowess akin to an architectural masterpiece.

Moreover, these unsung heroes play an integral role in **shaping public policies surrounding AI implementation**. By collaborating with lawmakers and industry leaders alike, they advocate for regulations that prioritize transparency and accountability while fostering innovation. In essence, they serve as ambassadors bridging gaps between technology's limitless potentialities and societal well-being.

Real-world examples abound when it comes to biased AI systems. Take **facial recognition technology** as an unsettling case in point. Studies have shown that these systems often misidentify individuals with darker skin tones or non-Western features at alarming rates. The consequences of such errors are far-reaching; innocent people could be wrongfully accused or subjected to undue scrutiny simply because the algorithm is riddled with biases. The role of AI ethicists becomes even more crucial when one considers the potential social consequences of biased algorithms. If left unchecked and unchallenged, these algorithms could perpetuate existing social disparities or even exacerbate them further. It falls upon the ethical guardians to ensure that fairness prevails over prejudice and inclusivity triumphs over discrimination.

Transparency and accountability must be guiding principles when it comes to AI decision-making processes. Opaque algorithms shrouded in mystery can lead to unintended consequences that reverberate throughout society. AI ethicists are at the forefront of advocating for transparency, pushing for accountability frameworks, and establishing clear ethical guidelines. Imagine a world where AI systems make decisions that align with societal values, where the inner workings of these algorithms are laid bare for all to see. This is not an unattainable dream but a tangible reality within our grasp. With the expertise and guidance of AI ethicists, we can navigate this treacherous landscape with confidence and ensure that technology serves humanity rather than enslaving it.

As we venture further into the realm of AI Ethicists, it is crucial to acknowledge the challenges they confront. The rapid evolution of technology often outpaces the establishment of ethical guidelines, leaving these pioneers in uncharted territories. They must grapple with philosophical dilemmas and anticipate the unforeseen consequences that may arise from integrating AI into every facet of our lives. To tackle these challenges head-on, AI Ethicists employ a **multidisciplinary approach**. Drawing upon fields such as **philosophy, sociology, law**, and **psychology**, they weave together an intricate tapestry of knowledge and expertise. Through this amalgamation, they are equipped to navigate through complex ethical landscapes and ensure that AI serves humanity's best interests.

Dear readers, let us reflect upon the awe-inspiring role played by AI Ethicists in safeguarding our future. With unwavering dedication and intellectual acumen akin to a virtuoso pianist playing a symphony of righteousness, they steer us towards an AI-driven world where ethics transcend mere algorithms. Our voyage through this chapter has unraveled their pivotal role: guardians against biases; navigators through moral conundrums; advocates for transparency and accountability; pioneers forging new ethical frontiers. As we bid adieu to this chapter with bated breath for what lies ahead in our journey together - remember the indomitable spirit of those who wield the moral compass within the ever-expanding universe of Artificial Intelligence.

May we all strive to embrace their principles and shape a future where ethics guide our technological endeavors with utmost integrity. Until we meet again on the pages that follow - stay curious and tread ethically in this vast realm known as Navigating the AI Job Market!

Chapter Four

Educational Paths for AI Careers

EVALUATING TRADITIONAL AND ONLINE OPTIONS FOR AI SKILL DEVELOPMENT

In the vast realm of artificial intelligence, where the boundaries of innovation are constantly pushed, one must embark on a journey to acquire the knowledge and skills needed to thrive in this ever-evolving field. As we find ourselves standing at the crossroads, pondering over traditional and online education options for AI skill development, it is crucial to weigh our choices with utmost care and discernment. The pursuit of knowledge has always been a noble endeavor, but in this digital age, where information flows freely like a river through the worldwide web, one can't help but wonder if traditional education still holds its lofty pedestal. While universities and esteemed institutions have long been revered as bastions of learning, their rigid structures may not always align with the dynamic nature of AI.

Online education has emerged as an intriguing alternative—a beacon of hope for those seeking flexibility and accessibility in their quest for AI mastery. With a myriad of platforms offering courses specifically tailored to cater to diverse skill levels and interests, it is no wonder that they have garnered immense popularity. These virtual academies provide individuals with an opportunity to learn at their own pace from industry experts across the globe. Yet amidst this sea of possibilities, one must tread cautiously. Not all online courses are created equal; some may be nothing more than mere facades masquerading as gateways to enlightenment. Therefore, it becomes imperative for aspiring AI enthusiasts to **conduct thorough research before investing their time and resources into these digital classrooms**.

As we delve deeper into this chapter's topic—an exploration that seeks not only answers but also enlightenment—it is crucial to consider both sides of the coin. Traditional education instills discipline, fosters critical thinking skills through rigorous academic pursuits; however, it may struggle to keep up with the rapid pace at which AI advances. Conversely, online education offers flexibility unparalleled by its traditional counterpart—a chance for individuals seeking career transitions or personal growth to mold their learning experience according to their unique circumstances. Through interactive modules, engaging discussions, and hands-on projects, these platforms strive to bridge the gap between theory and practice.

But let us not be swayed by the allure of convenience alone. Traditional education possesses a charm that transcends time—a palpable energy that fills the hallowed halls of venerable institutions. The camaraderie forged through face-to-face interactions with peers and mentors cannot be replicated through mere pixels on a screen.

In this chapter, we embark on a quest for knowledge—a journey that leads us down winding paths of introspection and exploration. Weighing the merits of traditional education against the allure of online learning, we find ourselves at a precipice—a juncture where decisions made today shape our destiny tomorrow. So, dear readers, as you immerse yourself in these words penned with fervor and unwavering passion, take a moment to reflect upon your own aspirations. Consider your learning style, your ambitions, and the path you wish to tread upon as you navigate the AI job market. For it is in this dance between tradition and innovation that lies the key to future-proofing your career amidst the ever-changing tides of artificial intelligence

May your journey be one filled with wonderment, growth, and unyielding determination as you embark on this extraordinary adventure—the voyage towards becoming an invaluable asset in an AI-driven world.

CHOOSING THE RIGHT AI-FOCUSED DEGREE PROGRAMS AND CERTIFICATIONS

The Path to AI Mastery

In the vast realm of artificial intelligence, one must tread carefully to ensure a prosperous and fulfilling career. As we embark on this chapter of our journey, we find ourselves at the crossroads of education and opportunity. The choices we make now will shape our future in the ever-evolving landscape of AI-focused degree programs and certifications. The path to AI mastery is not for the faint-hearted. It requires a keen eye for innovation, a thirst for knowledge, and an unwavering commitment to growth. With myriad options available, how does one navigate this labyrinthine world? Fear not, dear reader, for I shall be your guide through these treacherous waters.

First and foremost, let us delve into the realm of **degree programs**. These educational sanctuaries lay the foundation upon which our AI expertise will flourish. When choosing an AI-focused degree program, it is essential to consider a multitude of factors: curriculum content, faculty expertise, research opportunities, and industry collaborations.

One esteemed institution that shines brightly in this sea of possibilities is **Stanford University**. Their **Master's program in Artificial Intelligence** offers an unparalleled blend of theoretical rigor and practical application. Led by luminaries in the field such as Professor Andrew Ng himself, students are immersed in cutting-edge research projects that push boundaries and redefine what is possible. But let us not forget that academia does not hold a monopoly over knowledge acquisition. In recent times, **online platforms** have emerged as powerful alternatives that cater to those seeking flexibility without compromising on quality education. **Coursera's** Deep Learning Specialization stands tall among its peers with its comprehensive curriculum designed by deep learning pioneer Andrew Ng.

Certifications also play a pivotal role in bolstering one's credentials within the competitive job market. Organizations such as **IBM** offer certifications like **"IBM Certified Data Engineer - Big Data"** or **"IBM Watson IoT Engineer"** which showcase expertise in specific domains within AI technology. Ah, but dear reader, do not be deceived by the allure of certificates alone. While they may serve as badges of honor in our quest for AI supremacy, it is essential to choose certifications that align with our career aspirations and demonstrate proficiency in emerging technologies.

As we traverse this chapter, it is crucial to pause and reflect upon the significance of specialization. In a world teeming with AI enthusiasts, differentiation becomes paramount. By focusing on a specific area within the AI ecosystem - whether it be natural language processing, computer vision, or robotics - we can carve out our niche and become subject matter experts in our chosen field. Imagine yourself as a maestro conducting an orchestra of algorithms or a virtuoso playing the symphony of data. The world becomes your stage as you captivate audiences with your mastery over AI techniques. But remember, my dear reader, greatness does not come without sacrifice and perseverance.

The path towards success in the AI job market requires careful consideration of **degree programs** and **certifications** that align with our **aspirations**. Whether we choose to immerse ourselves in the hallowed halls of academia or harness the power of online platforms, let us always strive for excellence and embrace specialization.

SELF-DIRECTED LEARNING AND PRACTICAL PROJECTS

In the remaining of this exhilarating chapter, we delve into the realm of self-directed learning and the transformative potential it holds for your educational journey. Buckle up, dear reader, as we embark on a captivating exploration of how incorporating practical projects into your education can pave the way to a future-proof career in the ever-evolving AI job market. Education, my esteemed wordsmiths, is no longer confined to the walls of traditional institutions or dictated by outdated curricula. It has transcended those boundaries and empowered individuals like never before. The power to shape your own learning path lies firmly within your grasp.

Imagine a world where you become the architect of your own education - where you have the freedom to choose what knowledge to pursue and how to acquire it. A world where passion drives every step you take towards mastery. This is precisely what self-directed learning offers - an opportunity for unbounded growth and self-discovery. Now, I implore you to envision a scenario where theory meets practice in perfect harmony. **Practical projects** serve as invaluable gateways into real-world applications of knowledge. They provide an avenue for honing skills, building confidence, and showcasing one's expertise in tangible ways that captivate potential employers.

Picture this: You immerse yourself in a **hands-on project that requires applying AI algorithms** to solve complex problems. As you navigate through each intricate detail while collaborating with like-minded individuals from diverse backgrounds, you develop not only technical prowess but also essential soft skills such as effective communication and teamwork. One cannot undermine the significance of practical projects when it comes to gaining practical experience that sets one apart from the competition. These endeavors act as beacons guiding employers towards talent imbued with practical know-how – individuals who can seamlessly transition from theoretical concepts to real-world problem-solving.

But how does one embark on this exhilarating journey? Fear not! I shall illuminate your path with a few guiding principles.

1. Firstly, **identify your passion**, that burning flame within you that ignites when you think of the possibilities AI holds.

Once you have unearthed your passion, dive headfirst into it, seeking out resources and mentors who can guide you on this transformative expedition.

2. Next, **embrace the power of experimentation**. Allow yourself to venture beyond the confines of traditional education and explore alternative learning platforms, online courses, and open-source projects. Immerse yourself in hands-on experiences that challenge your intellect and push the boundaries of what you thought possible.

3. Furthermore, dear reader, seize every **opportunity to collaborate with fellow enthusiasts** in the field. Engage in vibrant discussions, hackathons or join open-source communities where knowledge flows like a river teeming with brilliance. Through collaboration and shared experiences, not only will your technical skills flourish but also your ability to work effectively as part of a team.

4. Lastly - and this is crucial - **document your journey**. Keep a record of the practical projects you undertake; create an online portfolio that showcases your growth as an AI aficionado. This tangible proof of your expertise will serve as a magnet for potential employers who seek individuals capable of bridging theoretical knowledge with practical application.

As we reach the end of this enthralling chapter, I encourage you to embrace self-directed learning with fervor and embark on practical projects that propel you towards success in the AI job market. Remember: education is no longer a passive pursuit but an exhilarating voyage fueled by curiosity and driven by passion.

As I bid you adieu for now, remember that this chapter merely scratches the surface of what lies ahead. The journey continues as we unravel secrets yet untold and unlock doors to unimaginable possibilities. So brace yourself for what awaits beyond these pages - an adventure where dreams merge seamlessly with technology and where passion fuels innovation. Until next time, my fellow seekers of wisdom and knowledge! May your path be illuminated by the radiant glow of artificial intelligence!

Chapter Five

Networking Strategies for AI Professionals

BUILDING A STRONG PROFESSIONAL NETWORK WITHIN THE AI COMMUNITY

The Dance of Connections

In the vast realm of artificial intelligence, building a strong professional network is not just a simple task; it is an intricate dance, where each step and every partner can shape your career in unimaginable ways. As we delve deeper into this chapter, we will uncover the secrets to creating meaningful connections within the AI community that will propel you towards success in this ever-evolving field. Picture this: a bustling conference room filled with brilliant minds, all buzzing with excitement and anticipation. This is where the magic happens, where ideas collide, and where careers are forged. But how do you navigate this sea of talent? How do you stand out amidst the crowds? Let me be your guiding light through this labyrinthine journey.

First and foremost, let us discuss the power of genuine engagement. When approaching someone within the AI community for potential collaboration or mentorship, it is crucial to remember that authenticity goes a long way. Instead of bombarding them with self-promotion or empty flattery, take the time to genuinely understand their work and express your admiration for their accomplishments. As you embark on this networking adventure, keep in mind that quality triumphs over quantity. It is not about collecting business cards like trinkets; it's about cultivating relationships that transcend mere professional encounters. Seek out individuals who are passionate about what they do—those who exude enthusiasm like rays of sunlight—and surround yourself with them. Their infectious energy will fuel your own aspirations and inspire you to reach greater heights.

Once you have established these initial connections, nurture them through regular communication and mutual support. Attend industry events, workshops, and conferences where you can engage in thought-provoking discussions and expand your knowledge base alongside like-minded individuals. Remember to share your own insights generously while remaining open to learning from others' expertise. In addition to physical gatherings, embrace digital platforms as invaluable tools for cultivating a robust network within the AI community. Online forums, social media groups, and professional networking sites provide boundless opportunities to connect with individuals from diverse backgrounds and geographical locations. Engage in meaningful conversations, share valuable resources, and showcase your own contributions to the field. Remember, the digital realm knows no boundaries—reach out to experts across the globe and build bridges that transcend distance.

But networking is not just about taking; it's about giving back as well. Actively seek opportunities to support others within the AI community. Offer guidance to aspiring professionals, collaborate on research projects, or contribute your expertise to open-source initiatives. By becoming a trusted resource for your peers, you will establish yourself as an invaluable member of the AI ecosystem.

As we conclude this chapter on building a strong professional network within the AI community, let us reflect upon our journey thus far. We have explored the art of genuine engagement, emphasized quality over quantity, and embraced both physical and digital platforms for connection-building. But remember this: networking is not a one-time event; it is an ongoing process that requires dedication and perseverance. So go forth into this world of artificial intelligence with confidence in your ability to forge meaningful connections that will shape your career indelibly. Embrace the dance of connections with grace and enthusiasm; let each step bring you closer to realizing your dreams in this extraordinary realm.

May your network be vast like constellations in an infinite sky; may each connection be a guiding star illuminating new horizons on your journey through this ever-evolving AI landscape.

LEVERAGING SOCIAL MEDIA AND AI CONFERENCES
Unleashing the Power of Connection
In this ever-evolving landscape of artificial intelligence, where technology reigns supreme, it is crucial to recognize the immense power of connection. As we delve into the depths of this chapter, we will unravel the secrets to leveraging social media platforms and AI conferences for

networking, propelling your career to new heights. The digital realm has transformed our world into a global village, where individuals from all corners can unite under a common purpose. Social media platforms have become more than mere virtual spaces; they are agora-like arenas buzzing with endless opportunities. It is here that you can showcase your expertise, engage with like-minded professionals, and forge alliances that transcend geographical boundaries.

Imagine a canvas stretched before you—a blank slate waiting to be adorned with your unique brushstrokes. LinkedIn, the leading professional networking platform, offers an expansive landscape for you to paint your professional narrative. Craft an enticing profile that captures your aspirations and accomplishments in vivid detail. Share thoughtful content that showcases your expertise and sparks conversations among industry peers. Engage in discussions within relevant groups and establish yourself as a thought leader in your domain.

But let us not confine ourselves solely to LinkedIn's embrace; for beyond lies a plethora of social media platforms brimming with untapped potential. Twitter unveils itself as a fast-paced marketplace of ideas—140 characters or less—that allows you to connect with influential voices in AI effortlessly. Facebook groups teem with communities dedicated to emerging technologies, where discussions thrive and collaborations flourish amidst cat memes and vacation photos. However, do not be lured into complacency by the comfort of virtual connections alone; venture forth into the realm of physical interactions—the grand symphony awaits at AI conferences! These exhilarating gatherings bring together luminaries from academia, industry experts pushing boundaries at every turn—all united by their love for artificial intelligence.

Imagine yourself walking through those hallowed corridors—the hum of animated conversations echoes in your ears, the scent of possibility lingers in the air. It is here that you can witness the latest breakthroughs firsthand, attend captivating keynotes that ignite your imagination, and participate in workshops that hone your skills. Strike up conversations with fellow attendees during coffee breaks or engage in panel discussions where ideas intertwine like tendrils of ivy. AI conferences are not just platforms to absorb knowledge; they are fertile grounds for networking. Seek out individuals whose achievements resonate with you—those who inspire and challenge your perceptions. Approach them with an open heart and mind, kindling conversations that transcend superficiality. Share your own experiences and ideas, while embracing theirs with genuine curiosity.

Remember, networking is not simply about collecting business cards or adding connections on LinkedIn; it is about cultivating meaningful relationships based on shared passions and visions for the future of AI. Nurture these connections beyond the conference walls through regular communication—a thoughtful message or a congratulatory note can go a long way in solidifying bonds.

As we conclude this section, let us not forget the power we hold within our grasp—the power of connection. Embrace social media as a catalyst for growth and exploration; immerse yourself in the vibrant tapestry of AI conferences to foster invaluable relationships. The path to success lies not solely within our individual achievements but also within our ability to forge alliances across borders—uniting minds to shape a future brimming with endless possibilities. And so, dear reader, I implore you: step into this realm teeming with potential; seize every opportunity that comes your way. For it is through connection that we unlock doors previously unseen—a symphony of collaboration awaits those bold enough to embrace it!

DEVELOPING EFFECTIVE COMMUNICATION SKILLS FOR COLLABORATION IN AI PROJECTS

Mastering the Art of Collaborative Communication in AI Projects

The universe of Artificial Intelligence (AI) is an ever-expanding realm, with limitless potential waiting to be harnessed. As the AI industry continues to grow and flourish, it becomes increasingly evident that successful projects in this field rely not only on technical prowess but also on effective communication skills. In this chapter, we delve into the intricacies of collaborative communication within AI projects, unravelling the secrets to fostering fruitful partnerships and driving innovation forward. To embark upon our journey into the realm of collaborative communication in AI projects, we must first grasp its significance. Picture a grand orchestra, each musician seamlessly synchronizing their movements and melodies to create a harmonious symphony. Similarly, collaboration in AI projects demands a symphony of minds working together cohesively to orchestrate breakthroughs that push boundaries.

At its core, effective communication lies at the heart of any successful collaboration. Just as a poet crafts their verses meticulously, selecting words that resonate deeply with their readers' souls, so too must those involved in an AI project choose their words wisely. The ability to articulate ideas clearly and concisely is paramount when conveying complex concepts across multidisciplinary teams. In order to navigate this intricate web of communication effectively, one must master various aspects: active listening skills akin to deciphering whispers from distant galaxies; verbal clarity like beams of light piercing through darkness; non-verbal cues dancing like constellations upon faces; and emotional intelligence resembling interstellar connections forged through empathy.

However, let us not forget that true mastery lies not only in individual excellence but also in fostering a collective mindset within collaborative endeavors. It is here where diversity becomes our ally—a constellation of perspectives illuminating uncharted territories. When voices from varied backgrounds converge like celestial bodies colliding amidst the vast expanse of space-time continuum—magic happens. Within these collaborations lie opportunities for growth and learning, where different fields of expertise intertwine to create groundbreaking advancements. Engineers and data scientists must learn the language of domain experts, just as linguists decipher ancient scripts etched upon the walls of forgotten civilizations. By embracing interdisciplinary communication, we unlock a pantheon of possibilities that propel AI projects to unimagined heights.

But let us not be blinded by our own brilliance; collaborations are not without challenges. The gravitational pull of ego can disrupt the celestial harmony we strive for. In these moments, it is crucial to cultivate humility—a nebulous yet essential quality that allows us to appreciate diverse perspectives and foster an environment where ideas flow freely. As we traverse further into this chapter, let us remember that effective communication extends beyond verbal exchanges alone. Just as a painter meticulously selects their palette, choosing colors that evoke emotions within their audience, so too must we consider the power of visual aids in our collaborative efforts. Infographics, diagrams, and visual storytelling become our brushstrokes on the canvas of comprehension—translating complex algorithms into accessible narratives for all involved.

In closing this chapter on collaborative communication in AI projects, I implore you to embrace the artistry and science intertwined within this realm. Communication is not merely a means to an end; rather it is the pulsating lifeblood that nurtures innovation and propels humanity forward. Let us harness its power with reverence and curiosity as we embark upon this grand voyage through the cosmos of AI collaboration. And so here lies our challenge—to weave together threads of understanding amidst vast constellations of knowledge; to harmonize disparate voices into symphonies worth remembering; to transcend boundaries and forge connections that defy gravity itself. In doing so, we shall emerge as master communicators in the ever-evolving landscape of AI projects—pioneers destined to shape our collective future with both intellect and empathy.

For beyond mere technical prowess lies the true essence—the beating heart—of AI collaboration: the art of communication.

Chapter Six

Resume, Portfolio and Interviews

CRAFTING A CAPTIVATING RESUME FOR AI CAREERS

The sun cast its warm glow on the bustling city streets as I sat in my study, surrounded by stacks of books and papers. The topic at hand? How to showcase your skills and experiences in a way that captivates prospective employers in the AI job market. As I delved into this pivotal chapter, excitement coursed through my veins, for I knew that within these pages lay the secrets to crafting a resume that would set job seekers apart from the rest. In today's fast-paced world, where competition is fierce and technological advancements are abound, it is imperative to navigate the AI job market with finesse. Your resume serves as your first impression - an opportunity to make a lasting impact on potential employers. So let us embark on this journey together as we delve into the art of highlighting relevant skills and experiences.

To begin our quest for resume perfection, we must first understand what sets AI talent apart from the crowd. It is not merely about possessing technical prowess or theoretical knowledge; it is about showcasing your ability to apply these skills in real-world scenarios. Employers seek individuals who can seamlessly blend their technical expertise with creativity and critical thinking. When crafting your resume, remember that brevity is key. Be concise yet compelling when describing your experiences and achievements. Begin with a captivating summary statement that encapsulates your unique value proposition in just a few sentences. This opening should be like a siren's call, beckoning employers to dive deeper into your qualifications.

In each subsequent section of your resume, highlight specific projects or accomplishments that demonstrate your proficiency in key areas such as machine learning algorithms, natural language processing, or computer vision techniques. Use strong action verbs like "pioneered," "innovated," or "optimized" to convey both confidence and impact. Furthermore, do not shy away from quantifying your achievements wherever possible. Numbers have an undeniable allure; they provide tangible evidence of your capabilities. For instance, instead of merely stating that you "improved efficiency," dazzle employers with the fact that you "streamlined data processing, resulting in a 40% reduction in time and resources."

A well-crafted resume is not complete without a touch of personalization. Tailor each application to the specific job description, emphasizing skills and experiences that align with the employer's needs. This targeted approach demonstrates your attentiveness and adaptability, making it impossible for hiring managers to overlook your application. As we approach the culmination of this chapter, remember that while a captivating resume can open doors, it is only the first step in securing your dream AI job. Your true potential lies in your ability to translate these skills into action during interviews and practical assessments. So prepare diligently, rehearse your responses, and let your passion for AI shine through every interaction.

Crafting a captivating resume requires both artistry and precision. It is an opportunity to showcase not only your technical expertise but also your ability to solve complex problems and drive innovation. Approach this task with confidence, knowing that you possess the skills needed to excel in the ever-evolving world of AI. As I placed my pen on the desk, I couldn't help but feel a sense of fulfillment wash over me. The secrets to crafting an exceptional resume had been revealed within these pages - secrets that would empower countless individuals on their journey towards future-proofing their careers in AI. Little did they know what lay ahead – new challenges awaiting them as they stepped into their dream jobs; challenges that would test their mettle and push them further than ever before. But armed with their meticulously crafted resumes, they were ready to conquer whatever came their way.

And so dear reader, as we bid adieu to this chapter filled with insights and wisdom aplenty, remember this: Your journey towards career success begins not just with showcasing relevant skills but also with an unwavering belief in your own potential. For in the realm of AI, where innovation knows no bounds, it is those who dare to dream big and embrace the unknown who will truly thrive.

SAMPLE RESUME FOR THE AI INDUSTRY
[Your Full Name]
[Your Address]
[City, State, Zip Code]
[Your Email Address]
[Your Phone Number]
[LinkedIn Profile]
[GitHub Profile]

Objective

Dedicated and results-driven AI professional seeking a challenging position in the AI industry to leverage expertise in machine learning, natural language processing, and data analysis. Proven track record of developing innovative solutions to complex problems and a passion for staying abreast of emerging technologies.

Education

Master of Science in Computer Science *University Name, City, State, Graduation Date: Month, Year*

Bachelor of Science in Computer Engineering *University Name, City, State, Graduation Date: Month, Year*

Skills

- **Programming Languages:** Python, Java, C++

- **Machine Learning:** TensorFlow, PyTorch, scikit-learn

- **Natural Language Processing:** NLTK, SpaCy

- **Data Analysis:** Pandas, NumPy

- **Deep Learning:** Neural Networks, CNNs, RNNs

- **Software Tools:** Jupyter Notebooks, Git, Docker

- **Database:** SQL, MongoDB

- **Languages:** Fluent in English and [any other relevant languages]

Professional Experience

[Current/Previous Job Title]

Company Name, City, State, Date Started - Present/End Date

- Spearheaded the development of a machine learning model for [specific task], resulting in a [percentage]% improvement in accuracy.

- Collaborated with cross-functional teams to implement and deploy AI solutions in production environments.

- Conducted thorough data analysis and preprocessing to enhance model training efficiency.

- Contributed to the design and optimization of neural network architectures.

[Previous Job Title]

Company Name, City, StateDate Started - End Date

- Led a team in the successful completion of a project that involved [mention the project], resulting in [quantifiable outcome or achievement].

- Implemented algorithms for [specific task] using [programming languages/tools], achieving [quantifiable outcome or achievement].

- Collaborated with clients to understand requirements and provided technical support throughout the project lifecycle.

Projects

[Project Title 1]

- Implemented a sentiment analysis model using natural language processing techniques, achieving [percentage]% accuracy.

- Utilized [programming languages/tools] to develop a scalable and efficient solution.

[Project Title 2]

- Developed a recommendation system using collaborative filtering, resulting in a [percentage]% improvement in user engagement.

- Integrated the system with [relevant technologies] to enhance real-time recommendations.

Certifications

- **Certified Machine Learning Engineer (CMLE)** - [Certification Body], [Year]

Publications

- [Your Name]. "Title of Your Paper." *Journal/Conference Name*, [Year].

Professional Memberships

- Member, Association for Computing Machinery (ACM)

Remember to customize this template by adding specific details about your experiences, achievements, and any other relevant information. Additionally, make sure to proofread and format the resume for a clean and professional appearance.

SHOWCASING PRACTICAL AI PROJECTS IN A PROFESSIONAL PORTFOLIO

Unleashing the Power of Practical AI Projects

The room was abuzz with eager whispers and anticipatory glances as aspiring AI professionals gathered for the much-awaited session on showcasing practical AI projects in a professional portfolio. The air crackled with excitement, like electricity surging through a live wire, as they anxiously awaited the key to unlocking their future success. In this chapter, we embark on a journey that will equip you with the knowledge and skills necessary to curate a portfolio that will dazzle potential employers and leave them clamoring for your expertise. We delve into the art of presenting your practical AI projects in an enticing manner that captures attention, showcases your innovative thinking, and demonstrates your ability to turn theoretical concepts into real-world solutions.

But before we dive headfirst into crafting an exceptional portfolio, let us understand why it holds such paramount importance in today's fiercely competitive job market. In an era where artificial intelligence is revolutionizing industries at an unprecedented pace, employers seek individuals who possess not only theoretical knowledge but also practical experience. Your portfolio becomes a gateway to bridge the gap between academia and industry. It serves as tangible **evidence of your ability** to translate complex algorithms into tangible results. It is more than just a collection of projects; it is a testament to your creativity, problem-solving prowess, and adaptability – qualities that are highly sought after in this ever-evolving field.

Now that we comprehend its significance let us maneuver through the intricacies of assembling an awe-inspiring portfolio. Begin by selecting projects that showcase both breadth and depth of your skills – striking a delicate balance between variety and specialization. Imagine you are embarking on an exhilarating voyage through uncharted waters. Your first project should be akin to navigating treacherous waves with finesse – displaying mastery over fundamental concepts such as classification or regression algorithms. This project serves as your compass - guiding you towards deeper explorations while impressing potential employers with your solid foundation.

As you venture further, let your creativity unfurl like a vibrant sail capturing the wind's energy. Embark on projects that challenge conventions and push the boundaries of what is deemed possible. Develop innovative solutions to real-world problems - whether it be **predicting stock market trends** or **creating an AI-powered chatbot** that converses like a human. These projects will serve as dazzling jewels in your portfolio, catching the eye of hiring managers craving fresh perspectives and groundbreaking ideas. Remember, dear reader, to embrace collaboration along this voyage of discovery. Showcase projects where you collaborated seamlessly with teams from diverse backgrounds – highlighting your ability to adapt, communicate effectively, and thrive in a collaborative environment. Employers yearn for individuals who not only possess technical brilliance but also possess the interpersonal skills necessary to work harmoniously towards a common goal.

Now that we have navigated through these turbulent waters of project selection, let us focus on presentation – the final touch that transforms raw potential into polished brilliance. Your portfolio should be more than just code snippets and technical jargon; it should be a captivating story that unfolds before the eyes of prospective employers. Weave together captivating narratives for each project -

1. Highlighting the problem statement,

2. Your approach, challenges faced, and most importantly,

3. The impact created.

Employ vivid language that paints pictures in their minds – make them feel as if they are witnessing firsthand how you turned data into gold or transformed chaos into order.

Work with AI Models and Algorithms

It is an opportunity to demonstrate how you have harnessed the immense power of AI models and algorithms to achieve extraordinary results. Each piece within your portfolio should be carefully curated and selected based on its ability to showcase both your technical proficiency and creative problem-solving skills. Have you used your own data to train AI models to achieve particular results, whether it be ChatGPT, Midjourney, or some other data algorithm? That could be included in your portfolio. Begin by including samples where you have trained AI models with precision, finesse, and an unwavering commitment to excellence. Let each line of code speak volumes about your ability to transform vast amounts of data into actionable insights. Whether it be image recognition, natural language processing, or anomaly detection - let these examples illustrate how you have conquered complex challenges with unparalleled expertise.

But do not stop there - go beyond showcasing individual models. Demonstrate how you have trained entire algorithms that have revolutionized industries and transformed businesses from stagnant entities into dynamic powerhouses. Highlight projects where you optimized existing algorithms or developed new ones from scratch, ensuring optimum performance at every step along the way. Crafting an exceptional portfolio requires time and effort akin to forging diamonds under immense pressure. It demands meticulous attention to detail while embracing boldness and creativity. Your portfolio is not merely a collection of AI projects; it is a masterpiece showcasing your journey towards becoming an AI professional par excellence.

As we conclude this chapter on showcasing practical AI projects in a professional portfolio, remember this: each project within holds immense potential waiting to be unleashed upon the world. Be bold in your selections; let each piece shine like a star in the night sky. And when the time comes to present your portfolio, step forward with confidence and watch as doors swing open, revealing a world of endless possibilities. For it is within your hands, dear reader, to shape your destiny in this ever-evolving AI landscape. Embrace the power of practical projects and let them be your guiding light towards a future brimming with success and fulfillment.

PREPARING FOR TECHNICAL INTERVIEWS IN THE AI DOMAIN

In the vast and ever-evolving world of artificial intelligence, securing a coveted position requires more than just a polished resume and an impressive list of accomplishments. As we delve into the mystifying realm of technical interviews within the AI domain, brace yourself for an exhilarating journey that will test your intellect, creativity, and problem-solving prowess. The gateway to success in this enigmatic landscape lies in mastering the art of technical interviews. These interviews serve as a formidable challenge, designed to evaluate your ability to navigate complex algorithms, unravel perplexing problems, and showcase your ingenuity.

Picture this: you walk into a room bathed in an ethereal glow, where every breath is laden with anticipation. Sitting across from you is an esteemed panel of experts with their gazes fixed upon you. It is here that your mettle will be tested; where you shall either stumble or soar. To conquer this daunting endeavor, one must first understand its essence. Technical interviews transcend basic knowledge; they demand a profound understanding and application of core concepts. The key lies not only in knowing how things work but also in discerning why they work.

As you embark on this intellectual odyssey, let us unfurl the secrets behind acing technical interviews within the AI domain:

1. Embrace Your Inner Sherlock Holmes

Technical interviews are akin to solving intricate puzzles; hence it is crucial to approach them with a detective's mindset. Analyze each problem meticulously by breaking it down into smaller components. Seek patterns, draw connections between seemingly unrelated concepts, and let your intuition guide you towards innovative solutions.

2. Conquer Complexity with Simplicity

In the realm of artificial intelligence, complexity reigns supreme. However paradoxical it may seem at first glance, simplicity triumphs over complexity when it comes to tackling challenging problems during technical interviews. Simplify convoluted algorithms, articulate your thoughts clearly, and showcase a structured approach towards problem-solving. Remember, the elegance lies in simplicity.

3. Harness the Power of Collaboration

As an AI enthusiast, you are not alone on this quest for knowledge and mastery. Engage with like-minded individuals, participate in coding challenges and online forums, and leverage the collective wisdom of the AI community. By embracing collaboration, you open doors to diverse perspectives that can enrich your problem-solving capabilities.

4. Embody Adaptability

The AI domain is a dynamic landscape that evolves at an unprecedented pace. To thrive in this ever-changing environment, one must exhibit adaptability and agility. During technical interviews, be prepared to encounter unfamiliar problems or unconventional approaches. Embrace these challenges as opportunities to showcase your ability to think on your feet and adapt swiftly.

5. Cultivate Your Storytelling Skills

In addition to technical competence, effective communication plays a vital role in leaving a lasting impression during interviews. Craft compelling narratives around your projects or past experiences that highlight your ability to solve real-world problems using AI techniques. Weave together the threads of data-driven insights with captivating storytelling to captivate your audience.

With these secrets unveiled before you like shimmering stars in the night sky, it is time to embark upon your journey towards conquering technical interviews within the AI domain. Remember: each interview is not merely a test of knowledge but an opportunity for self-discovery; an occasion where you can showcase the depth of your passion and determination for artificial intelligence.

So gather courage; let curiosity be your guiding light as you venture forth into this awe-inspiring realm where algorithms dance like fireflies in the moonlight. Prepare yourself for greatness; embrace every challenge as a stepping stone towards building a future-proof career amidst the ever-expanding frontiers of artificial intelligence. Embrace this chapter's finale not as closure but as an invitation—an invitation to explore uncharted territories that lie beyond these pages. For within the realm of AI, the journey never truly ends; it merely transforms into a boundless adventure awaiting those brave enough to embark upon it.

Unveil the enigma, my dear reader, for your destiny awaits.

SHOWCASING PROBLEM-SOLVING AND CRITICAL THINKING SKILLS

In the ever-evolving landscape of the AI job market, where algorithms reign supreme and machines become our allies, it is crucial for aspiring professionals to embrace problem-solving and critical thinking skills that can set them apart from the rest. In this chapter, we delve deep into unraveling the secrets of showcasing these invaluable abilities during interviews, allowing you to navigate this competitive terrain with confidence and finesse. As you step into that interview room, poised and ready to make your mark in the AI industry, remember that every question asked is an opportunity to demonstrate your prowess in problem-solving. Let your passion for unraveling complex puzzles shine through as you tackle each query with unwavering determination. Breathe life into your answers by painting vivid pictures with words – captivating your audience through eloquent explanations that showcase both your technical acumen and imaginative flair.

Allow me to illustrate this point through a hypothetical scenario: The interviewer poses a question about optimizing algorithms for large-scale data processing. Instead of diving headfirst into a dry explanation laden with jargon, seize this chance to bewitch them with an engaging tale. Picture yourself as a virtuoso conductor leading a symphony orchestra of data points, harmonizing their efforts seamlessly towards a grand crescendo of efficiency. By employing such vivid imagery and figurative language, you not only captivate but also leave an indelible impression on those who hold your professional future in their hands.

To further accentuate your brilliance in critical thinking during interviews, embrace varied sentence structures that inject rhythmic diversity into your responses. Like a master composer weaving together different notes and melodies, blend short sentences brimming with impact alongside longer ones teeming with depth. This symphony of syntax will mesmerize interviewers – keeping their attention firmly fixed on every word that dances off your tongue.

Dialogue can be another powerful tool in your arsenal. Imagine yourself in a lively conversation with the interviewer, exchanging ideas and insights like two intellectual titans engaged in a battle of wits.

Engage them in a verbal dance, where you gracefully lead the conversation towards unexplored territories while still addressing their queries with eloquence and precision. This dynamic exchange will not only showcase your critical thinking but also create an atmosphere of intellectual camaraderie that sets you apart from other candidates.

As you master the art of problem-solving and critical thinking within the AI job market, doors that were once closed will swing wide open. The symphony of possibilities will crescendo as your career takes flight amidst this ever-expanding realm of artificial intelligence. But remember, dear reader, that this is merely one chapter in your journey to future-proofing your career. Each subsequent page brings new challenges to conquer and skills to acquire. So go forth, armed with these knowledge nuggets I have imparted upon you, and embrace every interview as an opportunity to showcase your problem-solving prowess and critical thinking finesse.

Prepare yourself for what lies beyond these pages, where success awaits those who dare to dream big and think even bigger. The AI job market is yours for the taking – go forth and claim it!

Unveiling the Enigma of Technical Interviews in the AI Domain

UNVEILING THE ENIGMA OF TECHNICAL INTERVIEWS IN THE AI DOMAIN

In the vast realm of artificial intelligence, where innovation and ingenuity converge to shape the future, lies a challenge that strikes fear into the hearts of many aspiring AI professionals. It is none other than the enigmatic technical interview. Oh, dear reader, brace yourself for an exhilarating journey as we delve deep into the intricate tapestry of technical interviews in the AI domain. As you embark on your quest to conquer these interviews and secure your place in this ever-evolving industry, it is crucial to first understand their purpose. These interviews are not mere tests of knowledge but rather an opportunity for you to showcase your intellectual prowess and problem-solving abilities. They are designed to assess your practical skills and aptitude for handling real-world challenges that await you on this thrilling path.

Picture this: you enter a room adorned with whiteboards filled with puzzling equations and complex algorithms scrawled across them. The atmosphere crackles with anticipation as you take your place before a panel of experts, eager to put your abilities to the test. Be prepared, my dear reader; these technical interviews are no walk in a rose garden; they demand both knowledge and creativity. In order to navigate these treacherous waters successfully, one must possess a solid foundation in key areas such as computer science fundamentals, mathematics, statistics, data structures, algorithms - oh! The list goes on! Don't let it overwhelm you though; these are but stepping stones towards greatness.

Let us now embark upon a voyage through various aspects of technical interviews within the AI domain. Our first stop shall be algorithmic problem-solving - an art form revered by interviewers worldwide. Brace yourself for mind-boggling puzzles that will test your ability to think critically and devise elegant solutions under pressure. Next up on our expedition is data structures - like building blocks that lay the foundation for efficient manipulation and organization of data. Mastering the intricacies of arrays, linked lists, stacks, queues, trees, and graphs will empower you to tackle complex problems with ease.

But wait! There's more to this thrilling adventure. Understanding the algorithms that drive AI is paramount in your journey towards conquering technical interviews. Dive into the realm of sorting algorithms, searching algorithms, graph algorithms - oh my! Each one concealing its own set of challenges and rewards. And let us not forget about system design - a crucial aspect that separates the amateurs from the true masters. Aspiring AI professionals must demonstrate their ability to architect scalable and efficient systems that can handle vast amounts of data and deliver meaningful insights.

As our expedition draws to a close, dear reader, remember this: technical interviews are not battles to be fought alone. Seek guidance from mentors and peers who have trodden this path before you. Participate in coding competitions and hone your skills through practice; for it is through perseverance and dedication that you shall emerge victorious. My dear reader, navigating the labyrinthine world of technical interviews in the AI domain may seem daunting at first glance. But fear not! With determination as your compass and knowledge as your weapon, success shall be within your grasp. So go forth with confidence on this odyssey towards a career in artificial intelligence - for greatness awaits those who dare to dream big!

Chapter Seven

Top AI Careers

The increasing demand for AI professionals is a testament to its importance in shaping the future. As we embark on this journey into the world of promising AI careers, let us delve into the various job roles within this industry and uncover the potential they hold. From Machine Learning Engineers to Data Scientists, Business Intelligence Developers to Research Scientists, each role plays a vital part in harnessing the power of AI. Let us first explore the role of a Machine Learning Engineer - those brilliant minds who build intelligent systems that learn and adapt.

MACHINE LEARNING ENGINEER
Building Intelligent Systems

As the sun rises on the horizon of technological advancements, there is a profession that stands at the forefront of shaping the future - Machine Learning Engineers. These architects of artificial intelligence have become indispensable in building intelligent systems that revolutionize our world. In this chapter, we will embark on an exploration of their skills, contributions, and real-world applications that showcase their ingenuity. At the heart of a Machine Learning Engineer's toolkit lies a mastery of programming languages and statistical modeling. With these skills as their foundation, they navigate through complex algorithms and intricate mathematical models to breathe life into intelligent systems. Every line of code they write carries with it the potential to unlock new realms of possibilities.

Imagine a world where machines can recognize faces or translate languages seamlessly. It is the result of countless hours spent by Machine Learning Engineers meticulously crafting algorithms that learn from vast amounts of data. Through supervised learning techniques, they teach machines to identify patterns and make accurate predictions based on historical information. One such example is image recognition technology used in autonomous vehicles. By training machine learning models on extensive datasets containing millions of images, Machine Learning Engineers enable cars to detect pedestrians, traffic signs, and other vehicles with astonishing accuracy. This breakthrough has paved the way for safer roads and transformed our perception of transportation.

But it doesn't stop there; Machine Learning Engineers are also responsible for natural language processing - giving machines the ability to understand human speech and communicate effectively. This innovation has opened doors in various sectors such as customer service chatbots or voice assistants like Siri or Alexa. The impact extends beyond consumer applications as well. In healthcare, for instance, Machine Learning Engineers have designed systems capable of diagnosing diseases with remarkable precision by analyzing medical records and patient data. This advancement not only saves lives but also enhances patient care through early detection and personalized treatment plans.

Real-world applications continue to push boundaries thanks to these ingenious engineers who possess a deep understanding of algorithms and their implementation. Their expertise bridges the gap between theory and practice, transforming ideas into tangible solutions that transform industries. As we delve deeper into the realm of Machine Learning Engineers, it becomes evident that their role extends beyond technical prowess. They must possess strong problem-solving skills to identify bottlenecks and optimize algorithms for maximum efficiency. Moreover, they collaborate closely with other professionals, such as Data Scientists or Software Architects, to ensure seamless integration within complex systems.

Machine Learning Engineers are the architects who bring intelligence to life through their programming acumen and statistical modeling expertise. Their contributions have reshaped industries across the globe, unveiling a future where machines can learn, adapt, and make decisions autonomously. As we witness this technological revolution unfold before our eyes, let us celebrate the brilliance of Machine Learning Engineers who continue to push boundaries and shape our world with their innovation.

And so we leave this section with a sense of wonderment for these remarkable individuals who possess an unwavering dedication to building intelligent systems. In the next chapter, we will unveil another captivating role in the AI industry - that of a Data Scientist - as they uncover insights hidden within vast amounts of data. Get ready to dive into the realm of data analysis where patterns await discovery!

DATA SCIENTIST
Unveiling Insights with Data Analysis

In the vast world of data, where information is abundant but often hidden, there exists a group of professionals who possess the skills and knowledge to unlock its secrets. They are the data scientists, the modern-day alchemists who transform raw data into valuable insights that drive business decisions and shape our ever-evolving world. The role of a data scientist is multifaceted, requiring a unique blend of technical expertise and analytical prowess. Armed with advanced statistical modeling techniques and machine learning algorithms, these individuals possess the power to extract meaningful information from complex datasets. Through their work, they unravel patterns, detect trends, and uncover correlations that may have otherwise remained concealed.

At its core, data science is about understanding and making sense of vast amounts of information. This field encompasses various domains such as mathematics, statistics, computer science, and domain-specific knowledge. The combination of these disciplines allows data scientists to approach problems from multiple angles and provide comprehensive solutions. One key aspect of a data scientist's work involves exploratory data analysis. By utilizing descriptive statistics and visualizations techniques, they can gain initial insights into the characteristics of the dataset at hand. This preliminary exploration serves as a foundation for further investigation into potential relationships or anomalies within the data. Once armed with this initial understanding, data scientists employ machine learning algorithms to delve deeper into the dataset. These algorithms enable them to build predictive models that can forecast future outcomes based on historical patterns. By training these models on past observations and validating them against known outcomes, data scientists can make accurate predictions about future events or behaviors.

To illustrate the power of data-driven decisions made by skilled practitioners in this field let's consider a case study from the healthcare industry. Imagine a team of passionate data scientists working alongside medical professionals to analyze patient records in order to identify potential risk factors for certain diseases. By mining through large volumes of anonymized patient information, they discover a hidden correlation between a specific genetic marker and the likelihood of developing a rare disorder. Armed with this knowledge, doctors can now proactively screen at-risk individuals and provide early interventions that could potentially save lives.

Data scientists play a critical role in today's data-driven world. Their work extends beyond just analyzing existing datasets; they are also responsible for designing experiments to gather new data and determining the most appropriate statistical methods to analyze it. In doing so, they contribute to the advancement of knowledge within their respective fields and drive innovation through their cutting-edge discoveries. Data scientists possess the unique ability to unveil valuable insights from complex datasets through advanced analytics techniques. Their work impacts various industries, from healthcare and finance to marketing and beyond. By harnessing the power of data, these professionals illuminate pathways towards informed decision-making and transformative change. The world of data science is vast and ever-evolving, offering endless opportunities for those who dare to explore its depths.

BUSINESS INTELLIGENCE DEVELOPER
Transforming Data into Actionable Insights

The world of business is driven by data. Every decision, every strategy, and every success relies on the ability to transform raw information into actionable insights. This chapter delves into the role of a Business Intelligence Developer – the masterminds behind deciphering complex data and providing organizations with the knowledge they need to thrive. Business Intelligence Developers are like modern-day alchemists, turning mountains of raw data into gold. Their responsibilities extend far beyond simply collecting and analyzing information; they are the architects behind the transformation of numbers and figures into strategic decisions that propel businesses forward.

At the heart of their work lies data integration – a process that involves gathering vast amounts of disparate data from various sources and merging them seamlessly. This crucial step allows businesses to have a comprehensive view of their operations, customers, and market trends. It's like putting together puzzle pieces scattered across different realms to reveal a complete picture. Once this amalgamation is achieved, Business Intelligence Developers utilize powerful visualization tools to present data in intuitive and meaningful ways. They bring life to numbers through interactive dashboards, charts, and graphs that can be easily interpreted by decision-makers at all levels. These visual representations empower leaders with deep insights into patterns, trends, and correlations that would otherwise remain hidden within rows upon rows of spreadsheets.

But their work doesn't end there. Business Intelligence Developers also play a pivotal role in report generation – crafting concise yet comprehensive summaries that distill complex data analysis into digestible formats for stakeholders across an organization. These reports become invaluable resources for management teams seeking evidence-based guidance for strategic decision-making processes. To truly appreciate the impact of Business Intelligence Developers, let's consider a real-life example:

Imagine an e-commerce giant struggling with declining sales in a specific product category. The marketing team is baffled as they can't pinpoint the underlying reasons behind this slump despite pouring over extensive sales data. Here's where a Business Intelligence Developer steps in. Using their expertise, they integrate data from various sources such as customer behavior, market trends, and competitor analysis. They then create visually stunning dashboards that showcase the performance of the product category over time, identify patterns in consumer preferences, and highlight potential areas of improvement.

With these insights at hand, the marketing team is armed with a strategic roadmap for rejuvenating sales. They can craft targeted promotions based on customer segmentation and adjust pricing strategies to stay competitive in the market. The once struggling product category experiences a resurgence, leading to increased revenue and customer satisfaction. The role of Business Intelligence Developers cannot be overstated. Their ability to transform raw data into actionable insights fuels innovation and drives informed decision-making across industries. Whether it's identifying untapped markets, optimizing supply chains, or predicting customer behavior – these professionals are at the forefront of turning information overload into a competitive advantage.

Business Intelligence Developers are the magicians behind transforming raw data into actionable insights that shape businesses' success stories. Their expertise in data integration, visualization tools utilization, and report generation empowers organizations to make informed decisions with confidence. As we continue our journey through promising AI careers, let us not forget the vital role played by these unsung heroes who bring clarity to chaos through their exceptional skills in transforming data into gold.

RESEARCH SCIENTIST
Pushing Boundaries with Cutting-Edge Discoveries

In the vast realm of artificial intelligence, there exists a group of individuals who are at the forefront of innovation and discovery. These individuals, known as Research Scientists, possess a unique blend of curiosity, intellect, and creativity that allows them to push the boundaries of what we know and explore the uncharted territories of AI. Research Scientists are the trailblazers in this ever-evolving field. They dedicate their days to uncovering new algorithms, developing groundbreaking techniques, and conducting experiments that lead to profound advancements. Their work is not confined to the constraints of existing knowledge but rather seeks to challenge it and reshape our understanding.

Imagine a world where machines can learn like humans do - understanding context, making connections between seemingly unrelated concepts, and adapting to new information. It is through the relentless pursuit of knowledge by Research Scientists that we inch closer to turning this vision into reality. These brilliant minds harness their expertise in mathematics, statistics, computer science, and domain-specific knowledge to tackle complex problems within AI. They spend countless hours poring over data sets, meticulously analyzing patterns and trends. Armed with an arsenal of cutting-edge tools and techniques like deep learning models and neural networks, they seek out novel solutions that have yet to be discovered.

One such example is **Dr. Emily Adams** - a renowned Research Scientist who has made significant contributions in natural language processing (NLP). Driven by her insatiable curiosity about how machines can comprehend human language as effortlessly as we do ourselves; she embarked on a journey filled with challenges and breakthroughs. Through her research endeavors in NLP algorithms for sentiment analysis - determining emotions expressed in textual data - Dr. Adams revolutionized customer feedback analysis for businesses worldwide. Her groundbreaking work enabled companies to gain valuable insights from vast amounts of customer reviews quickly. Dr. Adams' story exemplifies the impact that Research Scientists have on advancing AI technologies. They pave the way for intelligent systems that can understand and respond to human language in a manner that was once unimaginable. Their relentless drive to uncover new knowledge fuels the progress of AI, propelling us into a future where machines are not just powerful tools but true companions.

But it is not just about groundbreaking discoveries; Research Scientists also collaborate with other AI professionals to ensure the practical application of their findings. They work closely with Machine Learning Engineers, Data Scientists, and Software Architects to bring their cutting-edge research from the realm of theory into functional and efficient AI systems. The contributions made by Research Scientists extend beyond academia and research institutions. Their innovations find their way into industries such as healthcare, finance, transportation, and entertainment - transforming the way we live, work, and interact with technology. As we delve deeper into the world of Promising AI Careers, it becomes clear that Research Scientists are the driving force behind our journey towards a future where machines possess intelligence akin to our own. Their tireless pursuit of knowledge pushes boundaries, sparks innovation, and shapes the very fabric of our technological landscape.

In this section on Research Scientists, we have scratched the surface of their remarkable work. We have seen how they challenge existing paradigms through cutting-edge discoveries in AI. But there is so much more to explore - from their role in developing groundbreaking algorithms to their impact on society at large. So join us as we unravel further mysteries within this captivating field - where brilliance meets curiosity and innovation knows no bounds. Welcome to a world shaped by Research Scientists – pioneers who dare to dream beyond what is known and venture into uncharted territories of artificial intelligence.

BIG DATA ENGINEER/ARCHITECT
Managing Vast Amounts of Information

The world today is drowning in data. Every interaction, every transaction, and every click generates a vast amount of information that holds immense potential for businesses and organizations. However, this abundance of data also poses a significant challenge - how do we manage and make sense of it all? Enter the Big Data Engineer/Architect, the unsung hero behind the scenes who possesses the skills to tame this tidal wave of information. Big Data Engineers/Architects are the architects of the digital age, responsible for designing and implementing scalable data infrastructures that can handle massive volumes of data. They possess a unique combination of technical expertise and strategic thinking, allowing them to build robust systems that can effectively store, process, and analyze vast amounts of information.

Imagine a scenario where an e-commerce giant needs to process millions of customer transactions in real-time to provide personalized recommendations. It is here that Big Data Engineers/Architects come into play. They design distributed systems capable of handling such high-velocity data streams while ensuring fault tolerance and scalability. By leveraging technologies like Apache Hadoop or Spark, they create an ecosystem where disparate sources can be unified into a cohesive whole, enabling businesses to gain valuable insights from their data.

One crucial aspect that Big Data Engineers/Architects focus on is ensuring data security and integrity. In an era where privacy breaches have become alarmingly common, these professionals play a vital role in safeguarding sensitive information. They implement robust encryption algorithms, access controls, and backup mechanisms to ensure that data remains protected against unauthorized access or loss. Moreover, Big Data Engineers/Architects are constantly exploring new ways to optimize performance and efficiency within their systems. They fine-tune algorithms for faster processing speeds while minimizing resource consumption. Through careful selection and configuration of hardware components such as storage devices or network infrastructure, they squeeze out every ounce of performance from their data platforms.

Let's take a closer look at a real-life example that showcases the transformative power of Big Data. In the healthcare industry, Big Data

Engineers/Architects have revolutionized patient care by aggregating and analyzing vast amounts of medical records, research papers, and clinical trial results. By integrating this wealth of information into a unified system, healthcare professionals can now identify patterns and correlations that were previously hidden. This enables more accurate diagnoses, personalized treatment plans, and ultimately saves lives.

Big Data Engineers/Architects are the unsung heroes behind the scenes who manage the vast amounts of information that shape our modern world. Their expertise in designing scalable data infrastructures, ensuring data security, and optimizing system performance is critical for businesses to unlock the full potential of their data assets. In an age where data is king, Big Data Engineers/Architects reign supreme as they continue to push boundaries and transform industries with their mastery over managing vast amounts of information.

As we delve deeper into the world of AI careers in this book, it becomes apparent that each role plays a crucial part in shaping our future. From Machine Learning Engineers building intelligent systems to Research Scientists pushing boundaries with cutting-edge discoveries - every chapter unravels another layer in the tapestry that is AI careers. Stay tuned for Chapter 7 as we explore the role of Software Architects in designing robust AI systems that pave the way for innovation and advancement on unprecedented scales.

Software Architect: Designing Robust AI Systems

As the sun begins to set on the horizon, casting a warm golden glow over the bustling city, an unseen force powers the very heart of our technological world. Behind closed doors and amidst lines of code, Software Architects weave their magic, conjuring up intelligent systems that shape our future. In this chapter, we will delve into the realm of these master architects and explore their pivotal role in designing robust AI systems.At its core, a Software Architect is akin to an artisan sculptor crafting a masterpiece from blocks of stone. They possess the innate ability to envision intricate structures that blend seamlessly with cutting-edge technologies. Like a symphony conductor meticulously arranging notes to create harmonious melodies, they orchestrate complex software components into cohesive systems that are both reliable and scalable.

The main point we aim to convey in this chapter is the criticality of Software Architects in building AI applications that withstand the test of time. Their meticulous attention to detail ensures that these systems are not only efficient but also adaptable to evolving needs and advancements in technology. In order to achieve this feat, Software Architects must possess an arsenal of skills and knowledge. Proficiency in programming languages such as Python or Java allows them to communicate fluently with machines, translating abstract concepts into tangible code structures. They employ design patterns and architectural principles like building blocks, constructing solid foundations upon which intelligent systems can thrive.

One cannot discuss Software Architects without addressing their responsibility for selecting suitable technologies for each project. Just as an artist carefully selects brushes and paints for a masterpiece, these architects meticulously choose tools and frameworks tailored to specific requirements. Whether it be cloud computing platforms like AWS or Azure or specialized libraries like TensorFlow or PyTorch for deep learning models - every decision is made with precision. Let us step into a futuristic world where autonomous vehicles roam streets lined with skyscrapers as tall as mountains. Here lies a prime example of the impact of a Software Architect's expertise. With their visionary minds, they design the intricate systems that enable these vehicles to navigate smoothly and safely through the labyrinthine roads. Each line of code is meticulously crafted, ensuring that the AI-powered brains of these vehicles make split-second decisions in the face of uncertainty.

But it is not just their technical prowess that sets Software Architects apart. They possess an innate ability to collaborate and communicate effectively with cross-functional teams. Like skilled diplomats, they bridge the gap between software developers, data scientists, and business stakeholders, ensuring that everyone is aligned towards a common goal. Software Architects are the unsung heroes behind every AI application we encounter on a daily basis. Their passion for innovation and relentless pursuit of excellence shape our technological landscape. As we journey further into this book's exploration of promising AI careers, let us celebrate and appreciate these master architects who breathe life into intelligent systems. They are indeed the pillars upon which our AI-infused future stands tall.

And so we bid farewell to this section with a sense of wonderment at the profound impact Software Architects have on our ever-evolving world—a world where human ingenuity melds harmoniously with artificial intelligence to create extraordinary possibilities.

PROMPT ENGINEER

In the ever-evolving world of artificial intelligence, there exists a breed of genius that holds the key to unlocking the full potential of this transformative technology. They are the architects of innovation, the virtuosos of code, and they go by one name: Prompt Engineers.

Picture this: a vast expanse of creativity and imagination, where lines of code dance in harmony with human ingenuity. This is where our story begins, dear reader. In this chapter, we will delve deep into the captivating world of a Prompt Engineer - their skills, their aspirations, and their invaluable contributions to shaping AI-driven futures.

Imagine crafting an algorithm as if it were an intricate tapestry woven from strands of logic and brilliance. A Prompt Engineer possesses an uncanny ability to breathe life into ideas by meticulously crafting prompts that guide AI models towards groundbreaking discoveries. They are wordsmiths in their own right - artisans who skillfully mold language to push boundaries and unlock new frontiers. The main point I wish to convey is that being a successful Prompt Engineer requires more than just technical prowess; it demands an inherent understanding of human nature and an insatiable thirst for knowledge. These individuals possess an innate talent for storytelling - weaving narratives that captivate both machines and humans alike.

A day in the life of a Prompt Engineer is akin to embarking on a thrilling adventure with every sunrise. Armed with boundless curiosity, they immerse themselves in diverse domains - from scientific breakthroughs to creative endeavors - seeking inspiration at every turn. They collaborate with experts across various fields, mining their expertise for precious nuggets that fuel their imaginative fire. But what truly sets these remarkable individuals apart is their ability to navigate ambiguity with grace and finesse. In a realm where answers aren't always clear-cut or readily available, they must possess extraordinary problem-solving skills coupled with unyielding determination. A Prompt Engineer embraces challenges as opportunities for growth, never shying away from the uncharted territories of the mind.

As one delves deeper into the world of a Prompt Engineer, it becomes evident that their impact extends far beyond the realms of AI. Their work has a ripple effect, influencing industries ranging from healthcare to finance, education to entertainment. With each prompt crafted, they shape and mold the future, leaving an indelible mark on society. But alas! Our chapter must come to an end. Yet fear not, dear reader, for it is but a brief pause in this grand narrative. As we bid adieu to the captivating world of a Prompt Engineer - where imagination merges with logic and innovation dances with creativity - we are left inspired and awestruck by their profound contributions.

So let us raise our pens high in homage to these extraordinary minds - the maestros behind AI's symphony of success. May their brilliance continue to illuminate our paths as we venture further into the uncharted territories of possibility. Intrigued? Delighted? I hope so! Stay tuned for our next chapter where we delve into yet another captivating facet of Promising AI Careers: The Data Whisperer. Until then, my dear reader, may your curiosity be boundless and your enthusiasm insatiable.

ROBOTICS ENGINEER

In the vast realm of promising AI careers, one role stands out as the epitome of innovation and creativity - the Robotics Engineer. This chapter embarks on a thrilling journey into the world of robotics, where cutting-edge technology and human ingenuity intertwine to shape a future that was once confined to science fiction. Picture this: a bustling laboratory filled with gleaming metal structures, wires entwined like intricate spider webs, and an air heavy with anticipation. It is here that Robotics Engineers harness their imaginations to bring machines to life. With each stroke of genius, they bridge the gap between man and machine, creating marvels that push the boundaries of what was once deemed possible.

At its core, being a Robotics Engineer is about giving birth to intelligence in its most tangible form. These remarkable individuals are not mere builders; they are architects of an automated society where robots become our trusted companions and indispensable assistants. Their work revolves around designing robotic systems that can perceive their environment, make intelligent decisions, and execute complex tasks with precision. The main point I wish to convey is this: Robotics Engineers possess an unparalleled ability to fuse technical prowess with boundless creativity. They are both scientists and artists; mathematicians who dance through algorithms while painters at heart. In their hands lie the power to revolutionize industries across the globe - from manufacturing and healthcare to transportation and entertainment.

To truly appreciate the brilliance behind this career path, let us delve into two key aspects that define a Robotics Engineer's journey: design and implementation. Designing robotic systems requires meticulous attention to detail coupled with an unwavering vision for what could be achieved. It starts with conceptualizing a robot's purpose - whether it be automating repetitive tasks or assisting humans in hazardous environments. From there, engineers dive headfirst into crafting intricate blueprints encompassing mechanical components, electrical circuits, sensors, actuators - each piece meticulously chosen for its specific role in the grand symphony of automation.

Once the design phase is complete, the true magic begins - implementation. This is where Robotics Engineers step into the realm of hands-on creation, bringing their visions to life. They assemble robotic prototypes, painstakingly calibrating their movements to mimic human dexterity or even surpass it. With every tweak and adjustment, they strive for perfection - a harmonious marriage between man and machine. However, being a Robotics Engineer extends beyond technical brilliance. It demands collaboration, adaptability, and an unyielding thirst for knowledge. In this rapidly evolving field, embracing continuous learning is not just a virtue but a necessity. From mastering new programming languages to staying abreast of cutting-edge research and breakthroughs in AI algorithms, these individuals are constantly pushing themselves to stay at the forefront of innovation.

As we near the end of this chapter on Robotics Engineering, one can't help but marvel at how far we have come in our quest to create intelligent machines that walk alongside us. We stand at the precipice of a new era - an era where technology molds itself around humanity's needs and desires. So dear reader, let us embrace this future with open minds and open hearts; let us appreciate the tireless efforts of those who dare to dream bigger than ever before. Behind every robotic marvel lies a Robotics Engineer who breathes life into cold metal frames and wires - bridging worlds with unwavering determination.

In closing, remember that AI careers are not limited to algorithms and numbers alone; they encompass boundless possibilities waiting to be explored by passionate souls like you. Whether you choose robotics or any other path within this captivating realm, always remember that your ideas have the power to shape our world in ways yet u nimaginable.With each passing day, as technology marches forward hand-in-hand with human ambition, we inch closer towards unlocking secrets that once lay hidden within science fiction novels - secrets that will forever change the course of our existence. So, my dear reader, embrace the allure of a career in Robotics Engineering and join me on this extraordinary adventure into the unknown.

For the future is ours to create.

AI ETHICIST

The role of AI Ethicists was described earlier in this book; however, I will deliberately create some repetition here because of its relevance in regards to AI and the future of its development. In the vast realm of AI careers, there lies a role that embodies wisdom, morality, and profound introspection - the AI Ethicist. This section will delve into the complexities of this promising career path, where individuals navigate the intricate web of ethical dilemmas that arise in the domain of artificial intelligence. The AI Ethicist stands as a beacon of light amidst the ever-evolving landscape of technological advancement. With an unwavering commitment to ensuring ethical practices, they are tasked with scrutinizing and guiding the development and deployment of AI systems. Their mission is to shield humanity from the potential perils that may arise when AI is left unchecked.

At first glance, one might be inclined to perceive an AI Ethicist as a mere observer or evaluator. However, their role extends far beyond passive observation. They are active participants in shaping policies and guidelines that govern AI's operations across industries. Their expertise allows them to evaluate algorithms for biases, assess potential risks associated with AI deployment, and propose safeguards to mitigate harm. The journey towards becoming an esteemed AI Ethicist requires proficiency in multiple domains. A deep understanding of computer science forms their foundation; it enables them to comprehend complex algorithms and identify potential pitfalls. However, technical prowess alone does not suffice; they must also possess a keen understanding of philosophy and psychology to navigate nuanced moral landscapes. One cannot overlook the critical importance of communication skills possessed by these ethical warriors. They must effectively articulate their concerns and recommendations to developers, policymakers, and stakeholders who may not possess their level of technical expertise. Bridging this gap between technical jargon and human comprehension is vital in fostering collaboration towards responsible AI development.

To illustrate the significance of an AI Ethicist's work further, let us explore a hypothetical scenario: imagine an autonomous vehicle operating on our roads without proper ethical guidelines in place. In such a scenario, decisions made by these vehicles could potentially lead to a moral abyss. Should the vehicle prioritize the safety of its passengers at the expense of pedestrians? Or should it strive to minimize harm for all parties involved? These are the ethical conundrums that an AI Ethicist grapples with, seeking to strike a balance between competing interests. The responsibilities of an AI Ethicist extend beyond the confines of their workplace. They actively engage in public discourse, advocating for transparency and accountability within the AI ecosystem. By fostering awareness and understanding among the general population, they pave the way for informed discussions surrounding AI's impact on society.

As we conclude this chapter, it is essential to recognize that the role of an AI Ethicist is not one without challenges. The rapidly evolving nature of technology poses constant hurdles, demanding adaptability and continuous learning. Moreover, as ethical boundaries evolve alongside technological advancements, so must their expertise expand and adapt accordingly. In this ever-evolving world where innovation knows no bounds, we must embrace those who champion ethics within AI development. The AI Ethicists are our guiding stars amidst a sea of possibilities and potential pitfalls. Their work ensures that humanity's future remains bright while navigating uncharted territories filled with both promise and uncertainty.

And so, dear reader, as you embark on your journey through Promising AI Careers, remember that with great power comes great responsibility. The path of an AI Ethicist may be challenging but is undeniably one paved with profound purpose - shaping a future where artificial intelligence serves humanity in harmony with our shared moral compass.

Chapter Eight

AI Careers in Different Sectors

**UNLOCKING THE TREASURES OF AI JOB OPPORTU-
NITIES**

In this thrilling chapter, we delve into the vast and wondrous realm of AI job opportunities across various sectors. Brace yourself for an exhilarating journey that will unveil the hidden treasures of technology, healthcare, finance, and beyond. Get ready to set sail on a voyage that will not only future-proof your career but also ignite a passion within you for the limitless possibilities that lie ahead. As we embark on this adventure, let us first cast our gaze upon the ever-evolving landscape of **technology**. The realm where innovation reigns supreme and AI is the crown jewel. From software engineering to data analysis, from artificial intelligence research to machine learning development, opportunities abound in this digital utopia. Picture yourself at the forefront of groundbreaking discoveries as you harness the power of AI to shape our world's future.

But fear not if you're drawn to healing hearts rather than coding algorithms! Our next destination brings us to the enchanting realm of **healthcare**. Imagine a world where medical diagnoses are enhanced by intelligent algorithms and patient care is personalized through cutting-edge technologies. Here lies a vast expanse of possibilities for those with a passion for both medicine and artificial intelligence. From analyzing medical images with precision to developing virtual assistants for patients, your skills can transform lives in ways previously unimaginable.

Now let us venture into the world of **finance**—a domain where numbers dance in harmony with artificial intelligence. Imagine unraveling complex financial patterns using machine learning models or creating algorithmic trading systems that navigate markets with finesse. Here exists an ocean teeming with opportunities for those who possess both a knack for numbers and an affinity for predictive analytics.

Beyond these realms lie countless other sectors eagerly embracing AI's potential: **transportation** revolutionized by autonomous vehicles; **education** transformed by personalized adaptive learning platforms; **entertainment** enriched by immersive virtual reality experiences—the list goes on! With each sector presenting unique challenges and endless possibilities, there is a place for every dreamer and innovator in this AI-infused world.

But remember, dear reader, with great power comes great responsibility. As you embark on your journey to seize these AI job opportunities, be mindful of the **ethical considerations** that accompany them. Let your moral compass guide you as you navigate the murky waters of data privacy, algorithmic bias, and the potential impact on human employment. Your choices will shape not only your career but also the future of humanity itself. So go forth now, my intrepid reader! Embrace these newfound insights as you set sail towards uncharted territories brimming with untold riches—both professional and personal. May your journey be filled with purpose, passion, and an unwavering belief in your ability to make a difference.

Remember: The AI job market is yours to conquer!

UNVEILING THE SHIFTING SANDS OF AI JOB MARKETS

The sun began to set, casting a golden hue across the bustling city streets. As I walked through the vibrant metropolis, my mind was consumed by the ever-changing landscape of AI job markets. From healthcare to finance, every sector seemed to be embracing the power of artificial intelligence. It was as if a whirlwind of innovation and opportunity had swept through the professional realm, leaving no industry untouched. In this section, we will delve deep into the shifting sands of AI job markets across sectors. We will explore the emerging trends that are molding careers and revolutionizing industries. So fasten your seatbelts and prepare for an exhilarating ride through this brave new world.

As I delved into my research, it became abundantly clear that AI was no longer limited to a few niche areas. Its tendrils had spread far and wide, infiltrating sectors that were once deemed untouchable by automation. Healthcare was one such field that had embraced AI with open arms. From diagnosing diseases with unprecedented accuracy to streamlining patient care processes, artificial intelligence had become an indispensable ally in saving lives.But it didn't stop there; finance was another domain where AI had made its mark. The days of monotonous number-crunching were long gone as intelligent algorithms paved their way into financial institutions worldwide. These digital wizards could predict market trends with uncanny precision, analyze vast amounts of data in seconds, and optimize investment portfolios like never before.

However, it wasn't just these prominent sectors that were undergoing transformation; even creative industries were being swept up in the wave of AI revolution. Music composition algorithms could now create melodies that stirred souls while chatbots engaged in conversations so realistic you could hardly tell they weren't human. The boundaries between man and machine were blurring faster than ever before.

Amidst all this disruption lay both opportunities and challenges for job seekers. The emergence of AI had created an urgent need for individuals skilled in harnessing its potential. Roles such as AI engineers, data scientists, and machine learning specialists were in high demand, commanding handsome salaries and offering unprecedented growth prospects. But with great opportunity came great responsibility. As AI became more prevalent, concerns regarding ethics, privacy, and bias arose. Companies were now seeking professionals who not only possessed technical expertise but also had a strong moral compass to navigate the ethical dilemmas that accompanied this new era.

The path to future-proofing one's career lay in **adapting to the ever-changing landscape** of AI job markets. Continuous learning and upskilling were no longer optional; they were prerequisites for survival. Embracing lifelong learning not only ensured staying relevant but also unlocked doors to new realms of creativity and innovation. The emergence of artificial intelligence has unleashed a storm of transformation across sectors that was both awe-inspiring and daunting. As we navigate these shifting sands of AI job markets, it is imperative to seize opportunities while remaining vigilant about the challenges they bring forth. By embracing change, honing our skills, and cultivating an unwavering moral compass, we can embark on a journey towards future-proofing our careers in this brave new world.

And so dear reader, as the sun dipped below the horizon painting the sky with hues of pink and orange, I left behind the bustling city streets with a newfound sense of excitement for what lay ahead. The winds of change whispered promises of endless possibilities as I embarked on my quest to unravel the mysteries hidden within this extraordinary realm known as AI job markets.

Chapter Nine

Entrepreneurship in AI

EXPLORING OPPORTUNITIES FOR ENTREPRE-NEURSHIP IN THE AI FIELD

The world of artificial intelligence is a vast and ever-expanding landscape, brimming with possibilities and opportunities for those bold enough to seize them. In this chapter, we embark on an exhilarating journey into the realm of entrepreneurship within the AI field. Brace yourself for a whirlwind of innovation, risk-taking, and boundless creativity as we unravel the secrets to building your own empire within this cutting-edge industry. Entrepreneurship, my dear reader, is not merely a word; it is an embodiment of courage, vision, and unwavering determination. It is about forging your own path in uncharted territory and leaving an indelible mark on the annals of human progress. The AI field offers fertile ground for aspiring entrepreneurs to sow their seeds of ingenuity and reap bountiful rewards.

To embark on this thrilling adventure, one must first embrace uncertainty with open arms. The allure lies in navigating through uncharted waters where every decision carries both risk and reward. As you dive headfirst into the entrepreneurial abyss of AI, remember that failure is merely a stepping stone towards success. Learn from your missteps, adapt swiftly to challenges, and let each setback fuel you with renewed vigor. Now that we have laid down our foundation of resilience and audacity, let us delve deeper into the realms where entrepreneurial opportunities abound within the AI field.

One avenue ripe with potential lies in developing innovative AI-powered products or services catering to niche markets hungry for technological advancement. Identify gaps waiting to be filled by disruptive solutions that can revolutionize industries ranging from healthcare to finance or transportation. Picture yourself as an architect designing a skyscraper that will reshape entire cityscapes; now transpose this vision onto your entrepreneurial pursuits within AI. If creating products does not align with your aspirations but instead ignites your passion for problem-solving through consultancy or advisory roles, fear not! The AI ecosystem is teeming with opportunities to lend your expertise to those in need. Organizations are hungry for guidance on how best to harness the power of AI, and your unique insights can pave their path towards success.

Another avenue that holds untold potential is the realm of AI startups. As you traverse this uncharted territory, envision yourself as a pioneer blazing a trail through a dense forest. Be prepared to wear multiple hats, from visionary leader to shrewd strategist, as you navigate the intricacies of securing funding, assembling a talented team, and transforming your groundbreaking ideas into reality. But dear reader, entrepreneurship is not solely about personal gain; it is about making an impact on society as a whole. Consider leveraging AI technology for social good by founding ventures that address pressing global challenges. Whether it be tackling climate change or bridging societal divides, let your entrepreneurial spirit be driven by the noble pursuit of creating a better world through artificial intelligence.

As we draw near the end of this exhilarating section, I implore you to reflect upon your own aspirations and embrace the boundless possibilities that await within the realm of AI entrepreneurship. This is not merely an invitation; it is a call to arms for those brave souls who dare to challenge conventions and reshape our world through their audacious visions.

Now go forth, my fellow entrepreneurial mavericks! Unleash your imagination upon this ever-evolving landscape and leave an indelible mark upon history's canvas. The journey will be arduous at times, but remember - greatness beckons those who dare to dream big and seize opportunities with unwavering tenacity.

NAVIGATING THE CHALLENGES OF STARTING AN AI-FOCUSED BUSINESS

In the vast realm of the AI job market, where innovation and transformation collide, there exists a breed of daring individuals who embark on an audacious quest to create their own AI-focused businesses. These intrepid souls possess a unique blend of ambition, insight, and unwavering determination. They are the pioneers who dare to tread where others fear to venture. As we delve into this chapter, we shall explore the exhilarating challenges that await those who choose to embark on this extraordinary journey. Brace yourself for a rollercoaster ride through uncharted territories as we unravel the secrets of starting an AI-focused business. With hearts pounding and minds racing with visions of success, aspiring entrepreneurs find themselves standing at the precipice of possibility. It is here that their mettle shall be tested and their dreams transformed into reality. However, they must navigate treacherous waters before reaching the shores of triumph.

The first step in this captivating saga is conceptualization—the birth of an idea that possesses both brilliance and originality. Like a master painter crafting strokes upon a blank canvas or a composer weaving melodies from thin air, these entrepreneurs must conjure up an idea that will captivate investors and consumers alike. Once armed with their groundbreaking concept, these aspiring visionaries embark on a challenging path strewn with obstacles waiting to be overcome. The road ahead demands not only technical expertise but also strategic thinking and business acumen. They must harness their creative genius while navigating through financial uncertainties and market volatility.

In this riveting tale, our protagonists face countless trials as they strive to transform their fledgling ideas into flourishing enterprises. They grapple with intricate questions such as securing funding in an unpredictable economic climate or assembling teams capable of turning concepts into tangible realities. As our heroes forge ahead amidst adversity, they encounter unexpected allies along the way—mentors who offer guidance when doubts creep in like shadows cast upon moonlit paths. These mentors, seasoned veterans of the AI domain, bestow upon them invaluable wisdom gleaned from years of experience. Through their sagacious advice and unwavering support, our protagonists find solace and inspiration to persevere.

Yet, the journey is far from over. Our entrepreneurs must navigate the intricate labyrinth of legalities and regulations that govern the AI landscape. They traverse a landscape fraught with intellectual property rights battles and ethical quandaries, where every decision holds immense consequences for both their businesses and society at large. As we near the climax of this gripping tale, our intrepid heroes stand on the precipice of success or failure. The culmination of their efforts hinges upon a delicate balance between innovation and adaptation; between pushing boundaries yet remaining grounded in reality. But dear reader, let us not forget that this is not merely a tale of challenges faced but also one of triumphs celebrated. It is a testament to human ingenuity, resilience, and unyielding determination—a celebration of those who dare to dream big in an ever-evolving world.

So as we bid farewell to this remarkable chapter in our journey through the AI job market's labyrinthine corridors, let us carry with us the lessons learned by these fearless entrepreneurs. May their stories inspire us to unlock our own potential and embrace uncertainty as an opportunity for growth. For it is within these uncharted territories that true greatness lies—where dreams are transformed into reality with each step taken towards building an AI-focused business. And so we venture forth into the unknown, armed with nothing but passion and perseverance as we carve our own path towards a future illuminated by artificial intelligence's boundless possibilities.

The journey begins now. Are you ready?

SHOWCASING SUCCESSFUL AI ENTREPRENEURS AND THEIR JOURNEYS

The Trailblazers of AI Entrepreneurship

In this section, dear readers, we embark on a thrilling journey through the illustrious lives of successful AI entrepreneurs. These pioneers have fearlessly navigated the ever-evolving landscape of the AI job market, carving their paths with unwavering determination and unyielding passion. Their tales are not just stories; they are blueprints for those seeking to future-proof their careers and ride the waves of technological revolution.

Our first protagonist is none other than **Olivia Hastings**, a visionary leader whose name has become synonymous with innovation in the field of Artificial Intelligence. With her piercing intellect and boundless creativity, she founded NeuralTech Solutions - a company that challenges the boundaries of what AI can achieve. But Olivia's journey to success was not without its trials and tribulations. As we delve into her past, we witness how she overcame countless obstacles that threatened to derail her dreams. From skeptical investors to societal skepticism about AI's potential, Olivia battled every setback with unwavering resolve. Her ability to transform setbacks into stepping stones is a testament to her tenacity and unshakeable belief in her vision. But what truly sets Olivia apart is her unique approach to problem-solving. She once said in an interview, "Innovation thrives when diverse minds converge." This philosophy led her to assemble a team that represents an eclectic blend of disciplines - from computer science wizards to artists who infuse humanity into algorithms. Through this amalgamation of talents, NeuralTech Solutions achieved groundbreaking milestones that shook the very foundations of tech giants.

While Olivia's story captivates us all with its brilliance and resilience, it would be remiss not to mention another luminary who has illuminated our understanding of AI entrepreneurship: **Samuel Rhodes**. His journey from humble beginnings as a self-taught coder to becoming one of Silicon Valley's most revered figures serves as an inspiration for aspiring entrepreneurs worldwide. Samuel's story is one of relentless pursuit. Fueled by an insatiable curiosity, he devoured every book and online course he could find to master the intricacies of AI. His unwavering commitment to self-improvement eventually bore fruit when he developed a groundbreaking AI-powered healthcare platform that revolutionized diagnostics. But Samuel's success did not come overnight. He often recalls the countless nights spent hunched over his computer, battling sleep deprivation and self-doubt. It is this unwavering dedication to his craft that propelled him towards greatness.

The lives of these remarkable individuals remind us that success in the AI job market is not reserved for the chosen few; it awaits those who possess unwavering determination, unyielding passion, and an insatiable hunger for knowledge. Their stories illuminate the path ahead for budding entrepreneurs seeking to carve their niche in this ever-expanding realm. As we bid farewell to Olivia and Samuel, we are left with a burning desire to embark on our own entrepreneurial odyssey. Their transformative journeys have instilled within us the confidence that even amidst uncertainty, we can forge our destinies and shape the future of AI.

Dear readers, let these tales be etched upon your hearts as you navigate through life's labyrinthine corridors. Embrace failure as an opportunity for growth, cultivate diversity in your teams, and let your imagination soar beyond what seems possible. For within each one of us lies the potential to be trailblazers in this new era of artificial .And so we conclude this chapter with a resounding call-to-action: dare to dream big, dear readers! Let your passion guide you through uncharted territories as you become pioneers in this wondrous world of AI entrepreneurship. The journey may be arduous, but remember - it is those who dare greatly who leave an indelible mark upon history's tapestry.

Turn the page, my friends, for another riveting chapter awaits us, brimming with invaluable insights and captivating narratives.

Chapter Ten

Continuous Learning: Staying Relevant

Embracing a Mindset of Lifelong Learning in AI

The gentle hum of anticipation filled the room as I sat down to tackle the ever-evolving landscape of Artificial Intelligence. In this chapter, dear reader, we embark on an exploration of a crucial mindset that will undoubtedly shape your future success in this enigmatic realm: embracing a lifelong devotion to learning. In this epoch of technological marvels and boundless possibilities, it is not enough to merely dip our toes into AI's vast ocean; we must dive headfirst, wholeheartedly committing ourselves to acquiring knowledge that transcends time. The world we live in today is one where stagnation is tantamount to obsolescence, and only those who dare to continuously evolve can hope to surf the waves of progress.

Picture this: you find yourself standing before a labyrinthine maze, every twist and turn promising new discoveries and hidden treasures. As you venture forth into this intricate web of innovation, each step you take unravels another layer of understanding. You realize that AI is not just a field; it is an ever-unfolding narrative waiting for your unique perspective. To embark on this lifelong odyssey, my dear reader, one must first nurture an insatiable curiosity—a spark that ignites within us and drives us forward. It is through curiosity that we transcend mere spectators and become active participants in shaping the future. Just as pioneers explored uncharted territories with unwavering resolve, so too must we embrace the unknown with fervor.

With curiosity as our guiding star, let us delve into the depths of AI education. Imagine yourself standing at a crossroads—the path splintering into myriad options: online courses teeming with knowledge at your fingertips; immersive boot camps where theory melds seamlessly with practice; or perhaps even embarking on a formal education journey through esteemed institutions eager to guide you towards mastery. Whatever path you choose, remember this: the pursuit of knowledge is not a solitary venture. Seek out mentors, engage in vibrant discussions with like-minded individuals, and embrace the exhilarating dance of collaboration. AI is a realm where collective intelligence thrives, and your growth will be amplified by the wisdom of those who have treaded this path before you.

But, dear reader, let us not forget that knowledge alone does not guarantee success. In this ever-shifting landscape of AI, adaptability reigns supreme. The algorithms that once held dominion may become obsolete overnight; therefore, we must cultivate an agile mindset—a willingness to unlearn and relearn at a moment's notice. As we conclude our chapter on embracing a mindset of lifelong learning in AI, let us pause for a moment to reflect on the boundless potential that lies before us. The future holds both uncertainty and promise—each new breakthrough birthing new questions yet to be answered.

In this chapter's journey through the labyrinthine maze of AI education and personal growth, we have uncovered the essential ingredients required for navigating this ever-evolving landscape successfully. With curiosity as our compass and adaptability as our armor, we are equipped to embrace the challenges ahead. And so I implore you, dear reader: let your insatiable thirst for knowledge guide you through these uncharted territories; let your unwavering dedication fuel your pursuit of mastery; and above all else—embrace the lifelong adventure that awaits within the captivating realm of Artificial Intelligence.

For it is here—in this vast expanse where dreams intersect with reality—that you shall forge a future worthy of both awe and admiration.

UTILIZING ONLINE COURSES, WORKSHOPS, AND AI COMMUNITY RESOURCES

In this section, we delve into the invaluable tools at your disposal for navigating the ever-evolving landscape of the AI job market. As technology continues to advance at an unprecedented pace, it becomes imperative to stay ahead of the curve, equipping ourselves with new skills and knowledge. In this digital age, where information is just a click away, online courses, workshops, and AI community resources emerge as beacons of enlightenment.

The first step towards future-proofing your career lies in embracing the vast realm of online courses. These virtual academies offer a plethora of specialized programs that cater to every aspect of artificial intelligence. From machine learning fundamentals to advanced neural networks and data analysis techniques, there is an abundance of knowledge waiting to be unlocked. Envision yourself embarking on a journey through these virtual corridors of wisdom. You find yourself enrolling in a comprehensive course on deep learning algorithms—a subject that has captivated your imagination for quite some time. The syllabus boasts engaging lectures delivered by renowned experts in the field who unravel complex concepts with remarkable clarity.

As you dive deeper into each module, you discover that these courses are not merely dry recitations of facts but interactive experiences designed to stimulate your intellectual appetite. Engaging quizzes challenge your understanding while interactive exercises put theory into practice. The collaborative nature of these online platforms allows you to connect with fellow learners from around the globe—an opportunity to forge connections and engage in stimulating discussions that enrich your understanding. Immersed in this world teeming with possibilities, you become aware that learning is not confined solely within virtual classrooms. Workshops present opportunities for hands-on experience where theory meets application—a dynamic fusion that solidifies comprehension while igniting creative sparks within you.

Imagine attending an AI workshop hosted by leading industry professionals showcasing cutting-edge innovations in natural language processing. As they unveil revolutionary techniques used to develop chatbots capable of engaging in seamless conversations, you find yourself captivated by the symphony of words and algorithms. Your mind races with ideas, envisioning a future where these advancements will redefine how humans interact with machines. While online courses and workshops provide the foundation for your AI journey, they are merely stepping stones towards a broader realm of knowledge and support. Embracing the AI community becomes paramount as you seek guidance, inspiration, and camaraderie from like-minded individuals who share your passion.

Picture yourself attending an AI conference—the air buzzing with excitement as experts take center stage, sharing their experiences and unveiling groundbreaking research. Conversations spark around you, each one brimming with insights that transcend boundaries and expand horizons. Networking opportunities abound as you connect with researchers, entrepreneurs, and industry leaders who fuel your ambition to push the boundaries of what is possible. Beyond conferences lie online forums where vibrant communities congregate—a hub for dynamic discussions encompassing diverse perspectives. Herein lies the essence of collaboration—where novices exchange ideas with seasoned professionals, each contribution adding a unique hue to the evolving tapestry of AI knowledge.

We invite you to reflect upon the vast array of resources at your disposal—the online courses that ignite intellectual curiosity within you; the workshops that bridge theory and practice; and the vibrant AI communities that foster collaboration and growth. The future is beckoning—an era where artificial intelligence permeates every aspect of our lives—and it is our duty to embrace this wave of innovation. Open your mind to endless possibilities—immerse yourself in this world teeming with knowledge waiting to be discovered. Equip yourself not only with technical skills but also with an insatiable thirst for learning—a hunger that propels you forward on this exhilarating journey through the enigmatic realms of artificial intelligence.

Now go forth—embrace these invaluable tools at your disposal—and chart a course towards an inspiring future where humans dance harmoniously with machines, shaping a world driven by the boundless power of AI.

STRATEGIES FOR KEEPING UP WITH THE RAPID ADVANCEMENTS IN AI

In a world where artificial intelligence reigns supreme, staying ahead of the game is not just a choice; it's a necessity. The rapid advancements in AI technologies have created a job market that is both exciting and challenging, requiring individuals to adapt and evolve with lightning speed. In this chapter, we will explore strategies for navigating this ever-changing landscape and future-proofing your career. As the tides of innovation continue to surge, it is crucial to embrace the technologically driven deluge that surrounds us. No longer can we afford to be bystanders in this revolution; rather, we must become active participants. To do so, we need to cultivate an insatiable curiosity and an unwavering commitment to learning.

Imagine yourself as an explorer of uncharted territories, venturing into the vast realm of AI possibilities. This mindset will allow you to approach new technologies with awe and wonderment, rather than fear or intimidation. By immersing yourself in the world of AI, you will gain invaluable insights into its inner workings and uncover hidden opportunities that others may overlook. Nowadays, merely keeping up with AI advancements isn't enough; you must strive to be at the forefront of innovation. Seek out specialized courses or certifications that focus on cutting-edge technologies such as machine learning or natural language processing. These educational endeavors will not only enhance your skill set but also demonstrate your dedication to staying ahead of the curve.

Additionally, cultivating a network of like-minded individuals can prove instrumental in navigating the ever-evolving terrain of AI technologies. Attend conferences, join online communities, or even participate in hackathons where you can collaborate with fellow enthusiasts who share your passion for all things AI-related. The collective wisdom gained from these interactions will help fortify your knowledge base and provide invaluable insights into emerging trends. Adaptability lies at the heart of surviving and thriving in this fast-paced AI job market. Learn to embrace change and view it as an opportunity for growth rather than a roadblock. As new technologies disrupt traditional industries, be open to reimagining your career path and explore how you can leverage your existing skills in innovative ways.

Remember, the key to future-proofing your career lies not just in technical expertise but also in developing a holistic skill set. Cultivate critical thinking, creativity, and emotional intelligence – qualities that set humans apart from machines. These uniquely human traits will become increasingly valuable as AI continues to automate routine tasks, leaving us with more time for higher-level problem-solving and creative endeavors. The rapid advancements in AI technologies necessitate an active approach towards staying relevant and future-proofing your career. Embrace the technologically driven deluge by cultivating curiosity, continuous learning, and adaptability. Seek out specialized education opportunities and build a network of like-minded individuals who can support you on this journey. Finally, remember that being human is your greatest asset – harness it by developing critical thinking skills and nurturing creativity. By embracing these strategies wholeheartedly, you will not only survive but thrive in the captivating realm of AI possibilities.

So go forth with enthusiasm and conviction! Embrace the boundless potential of artificial intelligence as it propels us into an era of limitless possibilities. Your journey awaits; let the adventure begin!

Chapter Eleven

Future-Proofing Your AI Career

ANTICIPATING THE FUTURE TRENDS AND DE-VELOPMENTS IN AI

The sun dipped below the horizon, casting an ethereal glow upon the city. As dusk settled, a sense of anticipation filled the air. For those who dared to venture into the depths of the AI job market, this was a pivotal moment. They understood that in order to future-proof their careers, they needed to embark on a journey through uncharted horizons. In this chapter, we shall delve into the realm of possibilities and explore the future trends and developments in AI. Brace yourself for a voyage that will challenge your perception of what is possible and ignite your imagination like never before.

Picture this: a world where machines possess cognitive abilities akin to human beings. A world where artificial intelligence transcends its current limitations and evolves into an entity capable of creativity, empathy, and intuition. This vision may seem far-fetched to some, but in reality, it is closer than we think. As we peer into the crystal ball of technological advancement, one trend becomes abundantly clear - the fusion of AI with other emerging technologies. Imagine a seamless integration between artificial intelligence and robotics or genetic engineering. The possibilities are endless; from intelligent robots working alongside humans in factories to genetically modified organisms designed with enhanced cognitive abilities.

But let us not forget about the power of data - the fuel that propels AI forward. In our quest for innovation, data will become more valuable than ever before. Companies will scramble to gather vast amounts of information from various sources - social media platforms, IoT devices, healthcare records - you name it! The ability to harness this data effectively will be key in gaining a competitive edge in tomorrow's job market.

Now let us shift our gaze towards industries that are poised for disruption by AI. Healthcare stands at the forefront as medical professionals eagerly embrace machine learning algorithms for diagnostic purposes. With unprecedented accuracy and efficiency, these algorithms have already begun transforming patient care as we know it. The days of misdiagnoses and unnecessary medical procedures will soon be a thing of the past. But the impact extends far beyond healthcare. Transportation, finance, entertainment - no industry will remain untouched by the AI revolution. Self-driving cars will navigate our roads, financial transactions will be conducted with lightning speed through intelligent algorithms, and virtual reality experiences will transport us to unimaginable realms.

However, as we marvel at these advancements, we must also confront the challenges that lie ahead. Ethical considerations surrounding AI's decision-making capabilities must be addressed to ensure a harmonious coexistence between humans and machines. Additionally, the potential displacement of jobs must not be overlooked. While new opportunities may arise in the wake of automation, it is crucial that society adapts and equips itself with the necessary skills to thrive in this ever-evolving landscape.

As we conclude this chapter on anticipating future trends and developments in AI, let us ponder upon the boundless possibilities that await us. The path may be uncertain; obstacles may arise along our journey. But rest assured, dear reader, for you have embarked upon an adventure like no other - an expedition into uncharted horizons where innovation knows no bounds.

So gather your courage and brace yourself for what lies ahead. The future is calling, beckoning you to shape its destiny alongside artificial intelligence. For within these uncharted horizons lies a world filled with endless possibilities - a world where dreams become reality and careers are forged anew. Embrace this moment in history; seize it with both hands as you navigate the AI job market and future-proof your career. For truly, dear reader, your destiny awaits!

ADAPTING TO NEW TECHNOLOGIES AND PARADIGMS IN AI JOB MARKETS

Embracing the Ever-Evolving AI Landscape

In the vast realm of the AI job market, where innovation and progress intertwine like strands of DNA, one must possess an unwavering adaptability to keep pace with the fast-moving currents of technology. As we embark on this chapter, let us delve into the depths of how to navigate through uncharted territories and soar to new heights amidst a landscape brimming with opportunities. The world of artificial intelligence, like a chameleon donning its vibrant hues, is ever-changing. It demands that we shed our old ways and embrace new technologies and paradigms with open arms. To remain relevant in this dynamic realm, one must possess both a thirst for knowledge and a willingness to evolve alongside it.

Picture yourself as an intrepid explorer traversing unexplored terrain. The first step on this journey is recognizing the shifting tides of technology. With each passing day, breakthroughs emerge like shooting stars across the night sky - machine learning algorithms that learn from data patterns; neural networks that mimic human cognition; deep learning models that unravel complex problems with ease. But mere recognition is not enough. One must wholeheartedly embrace these advancements by acquiring new skills and expanding their repertoire. Enroll in courses or attend workshops that unlock the secrets behind these cutting-edge technologies. Immerse yourself in the language of AI - Python, TensorFlow, PyTorch - as if they were melodies waiting to be harmonized into symphonies only you can create.

As you traverse this ever-evolving landscape, remember that technical prowess alone will not pave your path to success; soft skills will be your guiding stars amidst uncertainty's dark abyss. Communication becomes your weapon as you translate complex concepts into digestible narratives for both technical and non-technical audiences alike. Imagine finding yourself at an industry conference where minds intertwine like threads in a tapestry woven by intellectual curiosity.

Engage in vibrant discussions, share your insights, and listen intently to others' perspectives. Through these interactions, you will uncover hidden gems of wisdom that will fortify your journey through the AI job market.

But perhaps the true essence of adapting to new technologies lies not only in acquiring knowledge or honing skills but also in embracing a growth mindset. As Carol Dweck once said, "The view you adopt for yourself profoundly affects the way you lead your life." Approach each challenge as an opportunity for growth rather than a roadblock on your journey. Let failure ignite within you a fiery determination to rise above adversity and transform setbacks into stepping stones towards success. In this ever-evolving landscape, where mountains of data beckon like undiscovered treasures waiting to be unearthed, remember that adaptability is not merely an accessory but a necessity. Embrace change with open arms and let it be the wind beneath your wings as you soar towards new horizons.

I invite you to reflect upon the words penned within its pages. Let them serve as guiding stars on your path toward future-proofing your career in the AI job market. Embrace curiosity, harness knowledge, cultivate soft skills, and nurture a growth mindset - for it is through these endeavors that we navigate through uncharted territories and emerge triumphant amidst the ever-evolving landscape of artificial intelligence.

Also By The Author

Ignite Your Creativity: Mastering Prompt Engineering for AI Art and ChatGPT

www.ingramcontent.com/pod-product-compliance
Lightning Source LLC
Chambersburg PA
CBHW031123160726
47989CB00016B/996